75 Exceptional Herbs
for Your Garden

75 Exceptional Herbs
for Your Garden

Jack Staub

ILLUSTRATIONS BY
Ellen Sheppard Buchert

GIBBS SMITH
TO ENRICH AND INSPIRE HUMANKIND
Salt Lake City | Charleston | Santa Fe | Santa Barbara

First Edition

12 11 10 09 08   5 4 3 2 1

PUBLISHED BY
Gibbs Smith
PO Box 667
Layton, Utah 84041

ORDERS: 1.800.835.4993
www.gibbs-smith.com

DESIGNED BY Kurt Wahlner and Steve Rachwal
PRINTED AND BOUND in Hong Kong

Signed prints of the artwork in this book are available from the artist,
Ellen Sheppard Buchert, by contacting her at ellenbuchert@yahoo.com

Library of Congress Cataloging-in-Publication Data
Staub, Jack E.
   75 exceptional herbs for your garden / Jack Staub ; illustrations by
Ellen Sheppard Buchert. — 1st ed.
       p. cm.
   Includes bibliographical references.
   ISBN-13: 978-1-4236-0251-4
   ISBN-10: 1-4236-0251-X
   1. Herb gardening. 2. Herbs. 3. Herbs—Pictorial works. I. Title. II.
Title: Seventy five exceptional herbs for your garden.

SB351.H5S696 2008
635'.7—dc22
                    2008000721

For all our darlings
whose gifts were lost too soon—
would any of these
could have saved you for us

❧ Contents ❧

❦ Introduction ❦

"Happy the age, to which we moderns give
The name of 'golden,' when men chose to live
On woodland fruits; and for their medicines took
Herbs from the field, and simples from the brook."

—Ovid, *Metamorphoses*, Lib. XV

This has been a fascinating journey for me. Although I have probably cultured at least half of the herbs I offer to you in this volume, and have surely sought the comforting warmth of chamomile or lemon balm tea on a blustery day, chewed a sprig of parsley for refreshment, and noted the dynamic nutritive value of dandelions and such, my herbal acquaintance has mainly been in a culinary vein and, therefore, my medicinal knowledge sadly lacking. As a result, the multiple historic remedial applications to which most of these herbs have been subject have been a revelation to me, even those subsequently disproved by modern medicine, but particularly those whose ancient herbal employments have managed to retain their luster in the bright light of contemporary scrutiny.

It is entirely appealing to me to imagine a world in which there were no drugstores or pill manufacturers, so that it was to nature's pharmacy one was compelled to apply and, like the early herbalists, open one's eyes to experimentation, observation, and, ultimately, knowledge: pounding roots into poultices, distilling tinctures and decoctions from leaves and blossoms, brewing infusions, hanging fragrant boughs from doorways, strewing floors. Certainly there were many maladies that, in the end, would not be eased or cured by such treatments but, for all those, there were countless that could be—and still can be. A second joy in the composition of this volume was the identification of plants, growing probably not a hundred yards from my doorstep, which I have haphazardly noted and ignored as weedy presences during my years amongst our native Pennsylvania flora. They were and are available for numerous herbal and culinary tasks and, finally, I have the knowledge to avail myself of them.

Although I have generally eschewed any historically lauded herbs that lack modern application entirely, as mentioned, I have included a good number whose historic employments have been contemporarily modified, simply because the history and legend surrounding them is so fascinating and they are still attractive in the garden. One thing I was surprised to learn but which, ultimately, made sense was the importance of moderation in employment: to wit, a substance that in small doses might eradicate parasites or cancer or the effects of animal venom might potentially exterminate you in larger ones—such is the case with herbal constituents as benign as our common parsley or garden fennel. Therefore, ingestion of the concentrated essential oils of any of the herbs I mention here should be monitored most carefully. Another point of interest was the incredible antioxidant potential of some of these herbs, particularly those members of the mint clan containing carvacrol, thymol, and rosmarinic acid, or those plants rich in omega-3 fatty acids, these giving stunning new import to the idea of a comforting cup of herbal tea.

Occasionally in this book, I will stop to laud a plant but advise you to seek the herb (for instance, saffron) or the rendered oil at your local market or health-food store, as, while the plant itself may be comely in the garden, the processing of its herbal product is best left to someone else. On other occasions, I will counsel you to eschew planting the herb in question, as it is probably available in near weedy ubiquity in your local wild, and to seek it out there for its beneficial herbal applications.

But for most, I will urge you to both plant and employ it and, if you have the space for it, heartily endorse the construction of your own herb garden (light sandy soil, full sun) to decorate and scent your precincts, spice up your cuisine, and cure what ails you. In any event, I hope you will enjoy this journey as much as I have, and I wish you both exceeding good health and excellent dining along the way.

Jack Staub
Hortulus Farm
Wrightstown, Pennsylvania

ANGELICA

❧ 1. Angelica ❧
Archangelica officinalis (Angelica archangelica)

"Contagious aire ingendering pestilence
Infects not those that in their mouths have ta'en
Angelica, that happy counterbane . . ."

—Guillaume de Salluste Du Bartas, *La Sepmaine*, 1578

Who couldn't love an herb with the exalted sobriquet of "angel of the archangel?" A close, if supersized, relation to carrots, parsley, fennel, and celery in the greater *Umbelliferae* family, angelica, even before the dawn of Christianity, was regarded as a kind of cure-all "counterbane" against evil spells and enchantments. Although some botanists believe that angelica may be originally native to Syria, it has grown in frosty Iceland and Lapland since time immemorial, and an ancient Latvian ritual still involves an annual early summer procession in which Latvians bear armfuls of angelica, voicing chants so venerable that nobody knows their meaning. Angelica was thought to bloom on May 8, the feast day of St. Michael (the "Archangel" who delivered the glad tidings of the holy birth to the Virgin), and became closely associated with the Annunciation. A spray of angelica worn on St. Michael's Day is still thought to bestow near-universal healing and protection upon anyone who carries it.

Ultimately, angelica was held in such high religious esteem that it earned the additional appellation "Root of the Holy Ghost." John Parkinson, in his *Paradisi in Sole Paradisus Terrestris* of 1629, among many other uses, recommends a decoction of angelica for "swounings, when the spirits are overcome and faint, or tremblings and passions of the heart," and the dried, powdered root added to wine to "abate the rage of lust in young persons," which must have been happy news and of significant use to medieval parents. Nicholas Culpeper, in his *Complete Herbal* of 1653, maintained angelica root would "wonderfully help . . . the bitings of mad dogs and other venemous creatures," and Christopher Sauer, America's first herbalist, in his *Herbal Cures* of 1764, echoed far earlier sentiments when he noted, "When the winds of death are blowing, Angelica makes an excellent prophylactic against dangerous contagion . . ."

All this said, there is, unfortunately, little contemporary evidence to support these high-flown herbal claims, although angelica root still rates a mention in the Swiss, Austrian, and German pharmacopoeias, the Germans recommending it for indigestion and flatulence. German studies have also found that angelica root, either chewed or added as a powder to liquid or honey, relaxes the windpipe, and many modern herbals tout its effectiveness as a "stimulating expectorant," both, therefore, commending it for application in the treatments of colds and coughs and the like. However, angelica is employed almost exclusively culinarily, the stems candied for their sweet licorice flavor and the young leaves employed in teas and salads. It is also still common in Iceland to eat the roots raw with butter: your call entirely.

Far better to understand the majesty and sensory allure of this heroic honey-fragranced plant, with its many fennel-like joints, toothy pinnate leaves, large globe-shaped white-to-green umbels in June or July, and often growing to 8 feet tall or more, making it an absolutely fantastic ornamental idea for the back of a mixed border. Confusingly, angelica is commonly listed as both a biennial and a perennial, although it is really neither. A plant can take more than 2 years to mature and will often die after flowering and seeding, and its cycle is totally disrupted by cutting the flower stalks. That said, angelica is an immensely hearty sort that will enthusiastically self-seed in many situations and will stand up to brutalizing temperatures and sketchy soil situations with equal aplomb. Therefore, scatter a few seeds at the back of your border and stand back for the show. In the kitchen, try the peeled, chopped stems sautéed with an equal amount of chopped onion as a lovely aromatic accompaniment to a nice bit of roast pork.

❦ 2. Anise ❦
Pimpinella anisum

*"For the dropsie, fill an old cock with Polipody and Aniseeds and
seethe him well, and drink the broth."*

—William Langham, *The Garden of Health*, 1633

Anise, also known as aniseed, pimpinel, and sweet cumin, is a
member, like angelica, of the parsley family and, like many
umbellifers, is thought to be anciently native to Egypt, Greece,
and parts of the southern Mediterranean. According to excavated texts,
anise has been cultivated in Egypt since at least 2000 B.C., the flavorful
"seeds" having been employed as a diuretic and a digestive aid and to
relieve toothache. Anise is mentioned in the seventeenth-century-B.C.
works of Hammurabi, the sixth king of Babylon and author of the *Code
of Hammurabi*, one of the first legal treatises in recorded history, and it is
also known that Charlemagne adored this fragrant herb and planted it
extensively in his gardens at Aquisgrana (now the spa town of Aachen in
far western Germany) between 800 and 814 A.D. Anise was known to
British herbalists by the fourteenth century A.D., and, according to Mrs.
Grieve, was being cultivated in Great Britain by the mid-sixteenth century, when it was also introduced into South America by the Spanish *conquistadores*. The *Pimpinella* in anise's botanical name derives from the
Latin *dipinella*, or "twice pinnate," in reference to its leaf form, and
because of its pungent, licorice sweetness, anise saw broad medicinal
application across all cultures it touched, but particularly for respiratory
and digestive ailments.

Hippocrates, father of modern medicine, recommended anise for
respiratory issues in the fourth century B.C., and the Greek botanist
Dioscorides wrote in the first century A.D. that anise "warms, dries, and
dissolves" everything from an aching stomach and a sluggish digestion to
excessive "winde" and a stinking breath. John Gerard recommended it in
his *Herbal* of 1636 for "the yeoxing or hicket [hiccup]" as well as

ANISE

"strengthening the coitus," and in 1763 Christopher Sauer maintained that it "removes chill from the chest" and "staves off coughing fits." The "breath-sweetening" employment was also lauded by the British apothecary William Turner, who reported in 1551 that "anyse maketh the breth sweter and swageth payne." Interestingly, unlike many early herbal claims, most of those attached to anise are surprisingly smack on the money. We know now that anise seeds contain healthy doses of vitamin B, calcium, iron, magnesium, and potassium, as well as athenols, which aid in digestion, calm intestinal spasms, and reduce gas. A tisane made of anise has also proven effective in calming both coughs and chronic asthma, and, of course, anise is the main flavoring ingredient in those potent nectars anisette, pastis, and absinthe, the last of which will pretty much calm anything into submission.

Anise is also a very pretty plant, with bright green coriander-like foliage and lovely diminutive white-and-yellow flowers held in feathery umbels, the whole of it growing to about 18 inches. Anise seeds are actually the fruit of the anise plant, which, when dried, are transformed into those familiar gray/brown, longitudinally ribbed seeds habitually positioned as a *digestif* by the cash register in your favorite Indian restaurant. Anise is an annual herb and needs a longish, hot, dry season to seed successfully, so, in cooler climes, it is advisable to start seeds in pots indoors in March and set them out when the soil is well warmed up. Otherwise, sow seed *in situ* in dry light soil and a sunny spot early in April, thinning the plants to about a foot apart. When threshed out, anise seeds are easily dried in trays and jarred for future use. In ancient Rome, wedding celebrations customarily ended with an anise-scented *Mustacae* cake to aid digestion (and, one assumes, "strengthen the coitus"), so why not create your own festivity by mixing a handful of anise seeds into your favorite pound cake recipe?

❧ 3. Basil ❧
Ocimum basilicum

"With Basil then I will begin
Whose scent is wondrous pleasing . . ."

—Michael Drayton, *Polyolbion*, 1612–1622

It is fascinating to me that a plant as benignly loveable as our common sweet basil (*Ocimum basilicum*) developed in such a swirl of historical controversy and opposing symbolism. Thought to have originated in India, at least in the form of holy basil (*Ocimum sanctum*), basil is also incredibly ancient to both Africa and Asia, although the compact bush basil (*Ocimum minimum*) is native to South America alone. Basil is thought to have entered Greece with the returning armies of Alexander the Great in about 350 B.C., from whence it spread throughout the Mediterranean basin, ultimately reaching England and northern Europe in the early sixteenth century and the North American continent through the earliest Spanish explorers in the late sixteenth century. "Basil" seems to have two possible derivations: the first from the terrifying half-lizard, half-dragon *basilisk* of Greek mythology, famous for its fatally penetrating gaze (which seems to be where the negative connotations surrounding basil find their root), and the second from the Greek *basilikon,* meaning "royal" or "kingly," in reference to basil's regal scent and royal-purple flower wand. One ancient tale held that only a king was sufficiently highborn to harvest it, and then only with a sickle of gold.

In India, holy basil (*tulasi*) is regarded as sacred, being associated with the goddess Tulasi, who, after being tricked by Vishnu into betraying her husband and then killing herself, was worshipped ever after for her faithfulness, *tulasi* ultimately becoming a Hindu symbol of love, purity, and protection. Tradition still requires that the head of a Hindu believer be bathed in *tulasi* water before burial and a leaf placed on his breast to ensure safe conduct into the afterworld. In ancient Greece and Rome, however, it was bizarrely decided that basil would only grow well if you ranted and raved and shrieked wild curses while sowing the seed—one imagines this must have made spring planting in the southern Mediterranean a bona fide riot—and in France you can still hear the phrase *semer le basilic*, which translates to "sowing the basil," meaning "to rant and rave." Basil also developed a reputation for spontaneously generating scorpions: place a basil leaf under a flowerpot and presto—lift the pot to find one! This notion was further fortified when the seventeenth-century French botanist Joseph Pitton de Tournefort reported, "A certain Gentleman of Siena was wont to take the powder of the dry herb [basil] and snuff it up his nose; but in a short time he turned mad and died; and his head being opened by surgeons, there was found a nest of scorpions in his brain." Suffice it to say that, in many quarters, basil earned a reputation as a bearer of malice and lunacy, Chrysippus, the ancient Greek champion of stoic theory, reporting as early as the third century B.C.: "Ocimum exists only to drive men insane."

Then consider basil's most famous literary role, which occurs in Giovanni Boccaccio's fourteenth-century tale of the tragic Isabella and Lorenzo, most famously retold by John Keats in his "Isabella; or, The Pot of Basil." In the story, Lorenzo is murdered by Isabella's brothers and the clearly unbalanced Isabella decides, as a keepsake, to remove his head, pop it into a flowerpot, ". . . and cover'd it with mould, and o'er it set Sweet Basil, which her tears kept ever wet." On the lighter amatory side, in old Romania, if a girl presented her beau with a sprig of basil, they were officially engaged, and Italian suitors traditionally signaled their love by courting with a sprig of basil engagingly tucked into their locks—in many parts of Italy, basil still goes by the charming alter ego *bacia-nicola*, or "Kiss-Me-Nicholas." In the end, what is one to think? Nicholas Culpeper had a very clear idea when, in 1653, he deemed basil ". . . the Herb which all Authors are together by the Ears about, and rail at one another like Lawyers."

What seems beyond general contemporary debate, however, is that basil in any of its lovely scented forms is an easy-to-grow annual and a seasonal staple in the kitchen. There are many fine types from which to choose, and I always plant at least two varieties to spice up the summer table, with enough leftover come fall to process into pesto cubes and

BASIL

freeze for winter consumption. Some of the varieties that may be of interest to you are the classic big-leaved 'Genovese' type; the spicy 'Thai' variety with a hint of cinnamon; the tiny-leaved 'Globe,' perfect for pot culture; the sprightly 'Lemon' or 'Lime' types, scented with a hint of *Citrus*; and the purple and ruffled varieties like 'Red Rubin,' 'Opal,' or 'Purple Ruffles,' which add a becoming flash of color to the garden, although I have habitually found them more finicky of culture than the others. In any case, sow some seeds indoors in a pot or two on a sunny windowsill in early spring, set out when the weather warms up (or transplant into the garden) in a nice, sunny position and keep clipped, hoard a bit of fresh mozzarella, and wait patiently for the first garden tomato and the culinarily *n'est plus ultra* of a classic caprese salad.

✦ 4. Bay Laurel ✦
Laurus nobilis

". . . neither witch nor devil, thunder nor lightning, will hurt a man in the place where a bay-tree is."

—Nicholas Culpeper, *Culpeper's Complete Herbal*, 1653

The true culinary bay laurel (*Laurus nobilis*), also known as sweet bay, is antiquely native to the Mediterranean, India, and Africa alone, although its cousin in the greater magnolia family, the California bay (*Umbellularia californica*), also known as Oregon myrtle and pepperwood, is a close ringer but of a stronger savor. The ancient Greeks considered the *Laurus nobilis* both sacred and protective, and associated it with Apollo, who fashioned himself a crown of laurel to celebrate the slaying of Python, the tempestuous she-dragon of the underworld, upon whose former lair he built his Delphic temple and then roofed it with bay leaves to protect it from lightning. Similar celebratory wreaths were soon bestowed upon the winning athletes of the Pythian games at Delphi, ultimately graced the locks of the first Olympians, and were awarded to the greatest early poets—thus "poet laureate"—with our educationally esteemed *baccalaureate*, translating to "laurel berry."

Additionally, the Pythia, the anciently revered Apollonian Oracle of Delphi, is known to have chewed bay leaves to intensify her oracular hallucinations, famously delivered in an ecstatic trance, and partially induced by what contemporary historians now believe were ethylene vapors rising from fissures in the ground around her. Greek mythology also gives to this savory herb its Greek name *Daphne*, in reference to the beautiful nymph daughter of the river god Peneios and earth goddess Ge, whom they transformed into a bay laurel in order that she might escape the prurient advances of Apollo. From that moment on, the bay laurel was associated with purity, purification, and protection, with Nicholas Culpeper jumping onto the "protective" bandwagon in his *Herbal* of 1653 and attributing all kinds of pharmacological feats to the bay laurel,

Bay Laurel

including the berries being "very effectual against all poisons of venomous creatures" and the oil distilled from them helping with "palsies, convulsions, cramps, aches, trembling, and numbness of any part."

In a notable herbal leap of faith, the thirteenth-century Arab physician Ibn Baitar believed sporting a bay leaf behind one's ear could prevent inebriation; however, contemporarily, because of the bay laurel's strong camphorous fragrance, it is most generally herbally employed as an aromatherapy oil in the treatment of such complaints as colds, flu, and muscle aches. It is, however, its famous culinary merits that remain truly commendable. Additionally, *Laurus nobilis* is a handsome tree with signature thick, shiny, elliptical leaves, small pale-yellow flowers, and oval green berries, which will ultimately turn black in fall. That said, here I am forced to admit that the bay laurel is hardy only to USDA zones 8 through 10 and is a somewhat delicate creature, craving protection from frost (a good, thick mulching of its notably shallow root system) and wind (a sunny sheltered location), and requiring rich, well-drained soil. Leaves are also easily scorched by cold winds and weather but without cause for real alarm: new shoots will resprout handily in spring.

However, as many ancient households habitually displayed a "protective" potted bay beside the front door to ward off evil spirits, it is this employment I will recommend to the greatest number of you here. The bay laurel is a splendid candidate for pot culture and, loving a good spring pruning, may be kept to a manageable 6 to 8 feet tall as well as topiaried to suit your aesthetic whim. Just pot up in light well-drained soil, keep in a cool, dry, brightly lit spot indoors in winter, and move outdoors to a partially shaded locale in summer. Culinarily, what could be more entrancing than to harvest bay leaves off your very own tree (n.b.: leaves don't develop their full gusto until several weeks after picking and drying), tie them up with some fresh thyme and parsley, and add them to your favorite recipe in the flavorful guise of a classic *bouquet garni*. As Julia Child so aptly put it at the end of every television program: "*Bon appétit!*"

ॐ

❦ 5. Bergamot (Scarlet) ❦
Monarda didyma

Tea legend holds that, after the son of a Chinese mandarin was saved from drowning by an English soldier, Charles Grey, Prime Minister and Earl of the British Empire, was sent the gift of bergamot-scented tea, giving birth to the variety known forever after as "Earl Grey."

Certainly this is the story of a scent in search of a horticultural identity, as the term *bergamot* can actually refer to as many as three entirely different plant forms, linked only by the commonality of their strong lemony fragrance. What we might term "true" bergamot, although we will only touch on it here, is the bergamot orange (*Citrus bergamia*). Clearly a member of the greater *Citrus* clan and a Far Eastern native introduced to the Ivory Coast along the spice roads in the twelfth or thirteenth century, it was ultimately delivered into the Mediterranean by the sixteenth century, where it is still cultivated for its essential oil, a key ingredient in perfumes. "Bergamot" derives from the city of Bergamo in the Lombardy region of Italy, where the oil was first offered for sale, and it was the Italian Christopher Columbus who first carried *Citrus bergamia* to the New World from the Canary Islands in the fifteenth century. However, as its fruit is not possessed of the culinary distinction awarded many of its relatives in the *Citrus* family, the bergamot orange was not received with much interest and is still largely grown only in southern Italy and on the Ivory Coast for the fragrance industry. It is a typically handsome tree with star-shaped white flowers, glossy leaves, and fruit resembling a pear-shaped cross between an orange and a grapefruit. Bergamot essential oil, the scent of which is basically citruslike, is also described by knowing noses as being "fruity" and "warm, spicy, and floral," and is thought to be herbally effective in the treatment of depression, stress, and tension, as well as skin infections.

Another also-ran in the bergamot race is the American native orange

BERGAMOT (SCARLET)

mint (*Mentha citrata*), noteworthy for its distinctive citrus-like fragrance and dark green purple-tinged leaves often blushed with red on the undersides, the entire plant having a distinct reddish purple aspect in spring. Two other potential contenders in this fresh-fragranced group are our wild bergamot or purple bee balm (*Mentha fistulosa*), boasting lavender-hued flowers, and lemon bergamot, or lemon mint (*Mentha citriodora*), with strongly lemon-scented leaves and edible purple-pink flowers growing in whorls up the flower stalk. However, it is to our own native bergamot (*Monarda didyma*), also known as scarlet bee balm, gold Melissa, Indian nettle, and Oswego tea, to which we will turn our horticultural attention here. Scarlet bee balm is a beautiful perennial plant originally native to the Oswego, New York, area, notable for is blazing scarlet blossoms, and growing wild as far south as Georgia and as far west as Michigan. The plant's botanical name *Monarda* comes to us from the Spanish botanist Nicholas Monardes, author of *Joyfull Newes out of the Newe Founde Worlde,* published in Seville in 1569 and translated into English in 1577. As you might expect, "bee balm" derives from this pretty plant's remarkable attractiveness to bees (and hummingbirds). It earned the sobriquet "Oswego tea" from its popular employment by the Oswego Indians as a healthful and warming beverage, a usage they passed along to the earliest colonists who took to it with vigor, particularly in the wake of the Boston Tea Party, when real tea (*Camellia sinensis*) was a clearly politically incorrect alternative.

The Lakota tribe of North Dakota drank a tea made from the flower clusters of scarlet bergamot as a remedy for fevers and colds and a tea infused from the leaves for whooping cough and fainting spells, and they applied a poultice of the boiled leaves for eye pain. The Winnebagos of Nebraska employed a similar preparation for acne and other skin conditions, and the chewed leaves were placed on wounds to staunch blood flow. The Menominee of Wisconsin and upper Michigan infused the leaves and flowers into a tea to treat nasal congestion, and the Kiowas of Oklahoma and Texas soothed insect bites and stings with a mixture of crumpled scarlet bergamot leaves and saliva. A host of other Native American tribes, including the Blackfoot, Chippewa, Crow, Flathead, Navajo, Ojibwa, Teton, and Sioux, were also advocates of the virtues of

Oswego tea and employed it to treat everything from coughs and colds to fever, abdominal pains, and flatulence. The early Shakers, who settled near Oswego, New York, the birthplace of this popular plant, were also among its foremost champions, valuing scarlet bergamot not only for tea and culinary uses but also for the medicinal and antiseptic virtues of its essential oil in the treatment of bronchitis, sore throat, eczema, wounds, cramps, and urinary tract infections.

Although the crimson-blossomed *Monarda didyma*, growing wild in fields and on the banks of streams across much of the United States, is the most familiar of the *Monarda* family, here I will urge you to investigate some of your other bergamot options, as this statuesque perennial (growing from 2 to 4 feet) with its shaggy heads of tubular blossoms and mintily fragrant red-veined leaves is also available in colors ranging from pink and purple to white and lavender blue. All are possessed of that signature lemony scent, are hardy (to zone 4) and hearty almost to the point of weediness, are excellent for infusing teas and tisanes, and will certainly add vivacity and fragrance to any border. Some popular ones to look for are 'Croftway Pink,' with lovely soft pink blossoms, 'Marshall's Delight,' with hot pink flowers, and 'Blue Stocking' and 'Snow White,' with violet/blue and white blossoms respectively. Monardas are slightly thuggy in their spreading tendencies via rhizomes, so pay some attention in terms of border curtailment, and they will be most vigorous and floriferous if divided every 3 years or so. Dry the flowers for potpourris as they retain their color nicely, and the leaves for those healthful tisanes so dear to all early Americans.

✢ 6. Betony ✢
Stachys betonica (Betonica officinalis)

"Sell your coat and buy Betony."

—Ancient Italian proverb

Of all the herbs valued by ancient medicants, betony, a relation of the decorative border plant Lamb's Ear (*Stachys lanata*), is surely the most important one of which most of you have never heard. Also known as wood betony, bishopswort, purple betony, and lousewort, betony has grown wild over the meadows, hills, and heathlands of most of Europe and as far east as the Caucasus since predawn, and was once the sovereign cure-all of countless maladies, but most particularly "of the head," "betony" originating in the Celtic *bew* for "head" and *ton* for "good." Antonius Musa, physician to the first Roman emperor, Octavius Augustus, in the first century A.D., claimed that betony could cure 47 different illnesses, and Robert Turner, the seventeenth-century British physician, recounts 29 complaints for which betony was considered efficacious. John Gerard reports in his *Herbal* of 1636 that betony is ". . . good for ruptures, cramps, and convulsions . . . and is most singular against poison," and according to Mrs. Grieve in her *Modern Herbal* of 1931, betony was judged to be so effective an antique panacea that even stags wounded in the hunt were believed to search it out in the wild, and, consuming it, be cured.

Aside from its panoply of medicinal virtues, betony was also prized as a potent charm against evil and ill humors, being habitually planted in churchyards and hung about the neck as an amulet. Dioscorides reported in his *De Materia Medica* of the first century A.D that "the root borne about one doth expel melancholy and remove all diseases connected therewith," and the Dutch theologian Erasmus wrote at the turn of the sixteenth century that betony would protect "those that carried it about them," as it was capable of "driving away devils and despair" and being also ". . . good against fearful visions." The second-century Roman writer

BETONY

Lucius Apelius Thesius further reported: "It is good whether for the man's soul or for his body; it shields him against visions and dreams."

That, however, was then and this is now, and, not entirely unexpectedly, betony has taken a tumble from these exalted herbal heights and is no longer regarded as the cure-all of corporal and spiritual misery. However, modern herbalists still give it high marks in two historic quarters: treatment "of the head," i.e., headaches and facial pain, as well as in the "expellation of melancholy," i.e., to relieve nervous stress and tension, due to its glycoside content. Additionally, betony, being 15 percent tannin, is also still valued for its astringent properties in the treatment of diarrhea and irritations of the throat and mouth, an infusion prepared from the dried leaves being either drunk or used as a gargle, depending on the malady in question.

But also consider betony's attractiveness as a perennial plant, with pretty whorls of purple, pink, or white blossoms (although the wild wood betony is customarily a rich red/purple) held in interrupted spikes on square, ridged, nearly leafless stems erupting from a handsome tuft of green leaves, and usually growing to about 2 feet tall. Also commendable is its very hardy disposition (to USDA zone 4) and its ability to play nicely in almost any situation, and, in the perennial border, making an estimable and dependable midborder plant in a complimentary mix of blues, pinks, and whites. After flowering, cut betony down to the ground and a fine new crown of leaves will emerge. To employ herbally, tie up 6 or so stems in a fanlike arrangement and sling over a cord or hook until nicely dried, and then crumble the leaves and blossoms into an airtight jar. To make a nice de-frazzling cup of betony tea, pour a pint of boiling water over an ounce of the dried herb, let it steep for 15 minutes, find yourself a comfortable chair, and breathe deeply in between soothing sips.

ॐ

✤ 7. Bistort ✤
Persicaria bistorta (Polygonum bistorta)

In the north of England, bistort was historically known as "Easter Giant," a manhandling of "Easter Mangeant" (from the French manger, "to eat"), as it was anciently consumed during Lent in a bitter herb pudding.

Bistort is one of those herbs whose ancient herbal employment has happily survived the scrutiny of modern medicine relatively intact. A native of many parts of northern Europe, Siberia, Japan, and western Asia to the Himalayas, bistort has known a bevy of ancient descriptors, including "Snakeweed," "Easter Giant," "Adderwort," "Pink Pokers," "Twice Writhen," and "Pudding Grass." "Bistort" comes to us from the Latin *bis* or "twice" and *torta* meaning "twisted," in reference to the "twice-twisted" character of this interesting plant's root. It is this root that was herbally employed across many ages and cultures, commonly either dried into a powder or steeped into an astringent decoction with water or wine.

Nicholas Culpeper in his *Complete Herbal* of 1653 says of bistort: "The leaves, seed, or roots, are all very good in decoctions, drinks, or lotions, for inward or outward wounds or other sores; and the powder strewn upon any cut or wound in a vein, stayeth the immoderate bleeding thereof." The illustrious Dr. Herman Boerhaave, Dutch eighteenth-century founder of modern clinical instruction, recommended ". . . a decoction of it . . . for the fastening of loose teeth, diabetes, a too-abundant female relief . . . vomiting, diarrhea, and to prevent miscarriages," and in the early twentieth century, the always reliable Mrs. Grieve advises that bistort "seems to be one of the strongest of our vegetable astringents, and is justly commended for every virtue that has been ascribed to any other."

What we now know is that, containing about 20 percent tannin as well as gallic acid, starch, and gum, bistort's rhizomous root more than lives up to its antique reputation, making it one of the strongest astringent

BISTORT

medicines in the vegetable kingdom as well as highly styptic and, therefore, excellent for contracting tissues and staunching bleeding.

Black externally, red internally, and typically "twice bent" like the letter "S," a decoction of the bistort root makes a valuable gargle for the treatment of troublesome gums, canker sores, and sore throats, is a useful wash for burns and wounds, and may be taken internally to treat peptic ulcers, ulcerative colitis, and conditions such as dysentery and diarrhea. Parenthetically, its high starch content also made bistort root a historic food source in times of famine, when it was roasted, boiled in soup, or ground to make flour.

And if that were not sufficient glory, now consider this plant's virtues as a garden perennial of note, particularly in the guise of that lovely *habitué* of the border *Persicaria bistorta* 'Superba.' As decorative and stalwart a garden companion as you will find, 'Superba' boasts handsome clumps of 8-inch lanceolate leaves, bluish green above with a white midrib and gray tinged with purple underneath, from which rise slender stems with sheathed joints, each stem terminating in a dense, bottle-brush-like spike of striking pink flowers in summer, the whole plant growing to about 30 inches tall.

When grown in bold masses, there is absolutely nothing lovelier in a border, particularly when surrounded by blossoms of alternate form in complementary pastel tones, and they are similarly effective in fresh summer bouquets. Bistort prefers a somewhat damp situation but, that said, is extremely nontemperamental in terms of siting and pleasingly hardy to USDA zone 3. The signature twisty roots and rhizomes may be dug up in the autumn, cut longitudinally into manageable segments, and dried in the sun. To concoct an enviably all-purpose decoction, boil an ounce of the bruised root in a pint of water, cool, and sip or apply for what ails you.

❧ 8. Borage ❧
Borago officinalis

"Ego borago gaudia semper ago."
("I, borage, always bring joy.")

—Ancient Latin proverb

Native in some gauzy mist of time to the Aleppo region of Syria but now naturalized as a garden escapee in much of Europe and North America, borage has long been prized for its herbal, culinary, and decorative virtues. Some believe "borage" derives from a corruption of the Latin *cor*, for "heart," and *ago*, "I bring," in reference to this plant's legendary deliverance of "joy" or "courage" to whomever might sup on or sip of it. Due to its gray/green wooliness, borage was lumped by many early herbalists into the same category as bugloss (*Anchusa officinalis*) and alkanet (*Lycopsis arvensis*), causing some confusion in terms of each plant's designated herbal benefits. One fact, however, emerged eminently clearly: borage (*Borago officinalis*) seemed to make everyone happy—quite literally. In fact, it was Pliny the Elder himself, in his *Historia Naturalis* of 77 A.D., who first lauded borage's ability to ". . . maketh a man merry and joyful," and Sir Francis Bacon, English statesman and father of both the modern essay and the Baconian method of scientific deduction, writes at the beginning of the seventeenth century that borage ". . . hath an excellent spirit to repress the fuliginous vapour of dusky melancholie." John Gerard, in his *Herbal* of 1636, expounds on borage in this fashion: "Those of our time do use the flowers in sallads to exhilerate and make the mind glad . . . The leaves and floures of Borage put into wine make men and women glad and merry and drive away all sadnesse, dulnesse and melancholy, as Dioscorides and Pliny affirme. [Dioscorides and Pliny also maintained that borage was the famous *nepenthe* of Homer, which, when consumed in wine, induced blissful forgetfulness.]. Syrup made of the floures of Borage comforteth the heart, purgeth melancholy and quieteth the phrenticke and lunaticke

BORAGE

person." In the same century, John Parkinson commends borage ". . . to expel pensiveness and melanchollie," and John Evelyn, in his *Aceteria* of 1679, reports: ". . . the Sprigs in Wine . . . are of known Vertue to revive the Hypochrondriac and chear the hard student." Is everyone ready to order a case?

While modern medicine does not really substantiate this whole "joy," "revive," and "chear" thing, it does confirm that borage contains healthy amounts of potassium and calcium, the fresh juice affording about 30 percent and the dried herb about 3 percent of nitrate of potash. The stems and leaves are also excellent sources of saline mucilage, which, when cooked, also yields nitre and salt, and it is to these saline qualities that the historic invigorating properties of borage are currently pinned. As well, in 1985, widespread cultivation of borage in North America was begun for the purpose of harvesting borage seed, the oil of which contains 20 to 23 percent Gamma Linolenic Acid (GLA), almost twice as much as other sources. Research shows that GLA has huge potential in the treatment of the symptoms of rheumatoid arthritis. Now consider borage's distinctive woolly, gray/green, languidly drooping form growing in a stout rosette to 2 or 3 feet and its gorgeous star-shaped, bright blue blossoms with their signature black "beauty marks" (anthers, actually), and I believe we are on to something.

The flavor of borage is refreshingly cucumber-y, the leaves being excellent steamed or sautéed, the stems peeled and used like celery, and the fresh flowers showstopping in salads and, candied, on desserts. In medieval England, borage leaves were steeped in wine or cider with lemon and sugar to create a "cool tankard" and a little happiness on a sweltering summer eve. Contemporary astrologer and herbalist Jonathan Pearl, however, recommends this "joy"-full elixir to banish melancholy: loosely pack a blender with fresh borage leaves, pour in dry vermouth to cover, pulse into a green soup, let sit for 6 hours, strain, bottle, refriger-ate, and sip as your mood dictates.

❧ 9. Burnet (Salad) ❧
Poterium sanguisorba

"This is . . . a most precious herb . . . the continual use of it preserves the body in health and the spirit in vigor . . ."

—Nicholas Culpeper, *Culpeper's Complete Herbal*, 1653

Salad burnet (*Poterium sanguisorba*) vies with borage for the title of "happiest" of our herbal plants, as, although totally unrelated, both were esteemed historically for their cheering melancholy-banishing personalities and fresh cucumber-like savors. A member of the greater *Rosaceae* family, and native to most of Europe, northwest Africa, and southwest Asia, salad burnet has a notable although less tasty cousin in medicinal burnet (*Sanguisorba officinalis*), also known as "Great" burnet, and native to northern Europe, Asia, and North America. Closely related to the *Alchemillas* as well, *Poterium sanguisorba* was known by most ancients as *Pimpinella sanguisorba*, *Pimpinella* being a corruption of *dipinella*, in reference to salad burnet's twin pinnate leaves. William Turner gives this charming description in his *Newe Herball* of 1551: "It has two little leives like unto the wings of birdes, standing out as the bird setteth her wings out when she intendeth to flye." *Pimpinella*, however, now refers exclusively to the pretty though near-poisonous wildflower known as scarlet pimpernel, *Anagallis arvensis*, and salad burnet has been reassigned to the genus *Poterium*, which derives from the Greek *poterion*, or "drinking cup," describing its favored herbal application.

Although the family burnet was used for a fairly typical panoply of inward complaints and was also judged "a capital wound herb for all sorts of wounds, both of the head and body, either inward or outward" (Turner)—the botanical *sanguisorba* deriving from the Latin *sanguis*, "blood," and *sorbeo*, "to staunch"—it was as a consoling additive to a claret cup that really launched this food plant into the herbal pantheon. Parkinson relates in 1629: "The greatest use that burnet is put unto, is to

BURNET (SALAD)

put a few leaves into a cup with claret wine, which . . . giveth a pleasant quick taste thereunto, very delightfull to the palate, and is accounted a help to make the heart merrie." Dodoens conveyed in 1554 that "the leaves stiped in wine and dronken, doth comfort and rejoice the hart," and Culpeper asserts in 1653, ". . . two or three stalks with leaves put into a wine . . . are known to quicken the spirits, refresh and clear the heart, and drive away melancholy." Additionally, as noted, salad burnet was much valued as a "cool as a cucumber" ingredient in *sallets*, John Evelyn remarking that it was "a very common and ordinary sallet furniture," and reporting in his *Aceteria* of 1699 that salad burnet is ". . . of so chearing and exhilarating a quality, and so generally recommended . . . 'tis pass'd into a proverb: *'l'insalata non e' buon, ne bella, ove se non c'e' la pimpinella'* (the salad is neither good nor beautiful if there is no pimpernel.")

Sir Francis Bacon, father of the British Renaissance and proponent of both inductive reasoning and, apparently, unbridled sensuality—his mother, Lady Anne, famously lamenting his propensity for "welsh footmen one after the other"—recommended salad burnet to be set in allées along with thyme and mint "to perfume the air most delightfully, being trodden on and crushed." Salad burnet is a very pretty plant indeed, with its rounded fine-toothed leaves and crimson tufts of flowers, and is typically found growing nearly weedily in dry meadows in its native habitats. With the additional laudability of general unfussiness, hardiness to USDA zone 4, and an extensive root system that makes it exceptional for erosion control, salad burnet is also easily grown from seed or propagated by root division. Culinarily, the leaves, like many things one might entertain (as Sir Francis did), are best employed young and fresh, as they lose their cucumber-like coolness with cooking, so, if you have an herb garden, why not try a patch, pop some in a *sallet* (or even a claret cup), and see for yourself whether your load isn't lightened a bit?

❦ 10. Caraway ❦
Carum carvi

"Nay, you shall see my orchard, where, in an arbour,
we will eat a last year's pippin of my own graffing,
with a dish of caraways, and so forth . . ."

—William Shakespeare, *Henry IV*, Part II

araway (*Carum carvi*) is a biennial plant in the family *Apiaceae* and closely related to its feathery, prettily umbelled cousins anise, cumin, and dill. Caraway "seeds" (actually "achenes": dry single-seeded fruits that release their seed without opening) have been unearthed in prehistoric settlements in Switzerland dating to an impressive 4000 B.C., and many botanists believe caraway may constitute the most anciently employed spice on the European continent. "Caraway" appears to derive from one of three sources: from the ancient Arabic *karawya* or, according to Pliny the Elder, from *Caria* in Asia Minor, where he believed the plant originated, or, according to Dr. Fernie in his *Herbal Simples* of 1914, from the Gaelic *caroh*, a "ship," for the shape of the "seed"—your call entirely. The first mention of caraway seems to occur in the famed Ebers Papyrus of around 1550 B.C, and the caraway root is said to have constituted the nourishing *chara* of the Roman legions in 49 B.C., Julius Caesar reporting in chapter 48 of his *Civil Wars* that it was ". . . discovered by the troops which served under Valerius. This they mixed up with milk, and it greatly contributed to relieve their want . . ."

Dioscorides recommended doses of caraway seed oil for pale wan-faced girls in the first century A.D., and, in the seventeenth century, John Parkinson commented, "It is also made into comfites and taken for cold or wind in the body, which also are served to the table with fruit," while Nicholas Culpeper reported that "caraway seed . . . breaketh wind and provoketh urine . . ." and "the root . . . is pleasant and comfortable to the stomach, and helpeth digestion," also adding the external application of:

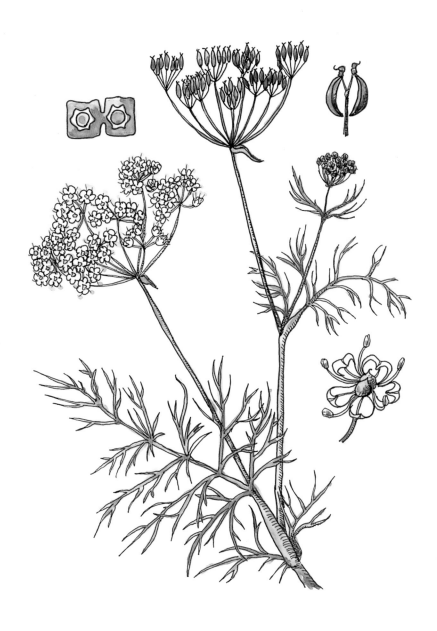

CARAWAY

"the powder of the seed put into a poultice taketh away blacke and blew spots of blows and bruises." Antique European legend held that caraway seed would prevent the theft of any object that contained it, and, in the same vein, was thought to keep both lovers and birds from straying, thus becoming a fashionable ingredient in both love potions and poultry and bird feed. The traditional English savory of a roasted apple accompanied by a dish of caraway seeds, which Squire Shallow offers to Falstaff in *Henry IV*, is offered to this day at the age-old Livery Dinners held by the Worshipful Company of Coachmakers and Coach Harness Makers of London.

As well, in Europe, the Middle East, and colonial America, caraway was used in the treatment of menstrual cramps, to promote menstruation, and to promote lactation in nursing mothers. Modern herbalists have identified carvone (40 percent to 60 percent) and limonene, two camphorlike compounds, as the active ingredients in the caraway seed's essential oil, both proven to soothe the smooth muscle tissue of the digestive tract and help expel gas. Additionally, as noted, caraway is a delicately appealing hardy biennial with frothy carrotlike foliage and umbels of tiny white-to-pink flowers blooming in early summer, the whole pretty plant growing to about 2 feet. Growing wild as it does throughout much of the world, caraway is a nicely carefree plant, and would be a smashing addition to a decorative herb garden, demonstrating only a preference for warmth, sun, and a well-drained soil. When the fruit ripens, separate by threshing, and then dry either on trays in the sun or on a cookie sheet in a low oven. The familiar dried brown seeds, crescent shaped with five pale ridges and their distinctive aniselike flavor, are truly wonderful as a *digestif,* so why not follow Squire Swallow's gentle suggestion and serve a dish of these pungent seeds as a time-honored accompaniment to a splendid roasted apple at the end of a meal? Surely Falstaff would approve.

ও

❧ 11. Chamomile (German) ❧
❧ 12. Chamomile (Roman) ❧

Matricaria recutita (Chamomilla recutita)
Anthemis nobilis (Chamaemelum nobile)

"Like a chamomile bed,
The more it is trodden
The more it will spread."

—Ancient English verse

This is a two-for-one idea, as here unfolds a *Prince and the Pauper*–like story of dual, nearly identical protagonists, although, in this *histoire*, there is also an immense cast of bit claimants, the name "chamomile" (or "camomile") having been applied to at least a dozen species in the *Asteraceae* family. However, generally and historically, only two were herbally employed, each, as in Mark Twain's tale, being hailed by various national clacks as the "true" variety, and one routinely being mistaken for the other. On one hand, there is what we call "Roman" chamomile (*Anthemis nobilis*), an aromatic creeper originally native to the Mediterranean and southwest Asia, the "Roman" idea having been bestowed upon it in 1598 by Joachim Camerarius, the German humanist and scholar, who, as you might expect, observed it growing in profusion near Rome. On the other hand, there is the "German" chamomile (*Matricaria recutita*), a sweet-scented plant native to the European continent and western Asia, in this pretender's case, the *Matricaria* deriving either from *matri caria*, "beloved mother," in reference to St. Anne, the mother of the Virgin and patron saint of both women in labor and miners, to whom this plant is dedicated, or from *matrix*, "womb," describing its ancient employment for female complaints.

"Chamomile" comes to us from the Greek *khamai*, "on the ground," and *melo*, "apple" or "melon," thus "ground apple," referring to Roman chamomile's low-growing habit and applelike scent, Pliny the Elder

CHAMOMILE (GERMAN)

describing the plant as having the aroma of "apples or quinces." Roman chamomile has been naturalized in England since the Dark Ages, is mentioned under the sobriquet "Maythen" in the eleventh-century Anglo-Saxon *Lacnunga* ("Remedies"), and is the "true" chamomile of the British Isles, constituting one of the early Saxons' nine sacred herbs. Semiparenthetically, during the Middle Ages in Britain, *Anthemis nobilis* gave birth to two of its most significant spawns: the double-flowered though sadly sterile 'Flora Pleno' type (must be propagated from sets), and the blossomless county Cornwall native 'Trenague,' immensely popular as a dense, aromatic lawn plant (the ancient verse above referring to this particular form). *Matricaria recutita*, the German chamomile, is held by its supporters to be the "true" chamomile of continental Europe, and is also widely naturalized in the United States. The truth is that there are marked similarities between these two claimants to the "true" chamomile crown—such as fine, feathery green foliage and white daisy-like flowers with yellow centers—the main difference being their growth habits, Roman chamomile being perennial and forming a dense, scantily blossomed low mat, and German chamomile being an annual (although happily self-seeding), with a looser, multibranched and blossomed clumping habit to about 2 feet. Additionally, physiognomically, the receptacle of the compound flower head of the German type is hollow, while the Roman is not.

Just to confound matters further, the "chamomiles," while being profoundly different in chemical components, were almost identically employed herbally, having been used as "strewing" herbs, sleep aids, treatments for fevers, colds, and stomach ailments, complaints "of the mother," and as anti-inflammatories, as well as externally as a compress for sciatica, gout, lumbago, rheumatism, and skin ailments. Chamomile was so venerated in ancient Egypt that it was employed as a cure-all for the "ague" and dedicated to the sun god Ra. Nicholas Culpeper claimed of the Roman type that "it is profitable for all sorts of agues . . . and there is nothing more profitable to the sides and regions of the spleen and liver than it: the bathing with a decoction of camomile takes away weariness, eases pains, to what part of the body soever they be applied." Meanwhile, at about the same moment, back on the continent, German chamomile was so highly prized as an herbal remedy in its namesake country that it earned the title *alles zutraut*, meaning "capable of anything." Dr. W. T. Fernie, in his *Herbal Simples* of 1914, in this instance referring to the Roman variety, maintains: "No Simple in the whole catalogue of herbal medicines is possessed of a quality more friendly and beneficial to the intestines than Chamomile flowers."

As noted, each of these plants is possessed of an entirely different chemical makeup: alpha-bisabolol and azulenes being the main components of the German type; amyl butyrate and butyl- and amyl angelate of the Roman. Research has confirmed many of the traditional uses of these plants, and chamomile is included in the pharmacopoeias of 26 different countries, and is still widely employed as an antipeptic, antispasmodic, antibacterial, antifungal, and antiallergenic idea. Additionally, the Herb Research Foundation in Boulder, Colorado, estimates that, worldwide, over a million comforting cups of chamomile tea are consumed each day, most probably making it the most widely consumed herbal tea on the planet. A few cautions, however: while teas and tisanes are benign substances, chamomile's essential oil (a wonderful blue color) is potent and should not be ingested without medical supervision or taken during pregnancy. Also, oddly, although a proven antiallergin, chamomile may cause hayfever-like symptoms in individuals allergic to ragweed.

In an interesting sidebar, medieval monks were astonished by Roman chamomile's beneficent effect on ailing plants when planted nearby, giving birth to *Anthemis nobilis*'s reputation as "The Plant's Physician," Frances A. Bardswell stating in her *Herb Garden* of 1911 that "nothing will keep a garden so healthy as plenty of Camomile . . . It will even revive drooping and sickly plants if placed near them." As noted, Roman chamomile is perennial, easy to propagate from seed with the exception of the 'Flora Pleno' variety, and hardy to USDA zone 3. For lawns of this summer-flowering herb (or search out the flowerless 'Trenague' type), space plants 12 inches apart and tread them in firmly: just as in the old verse, it will not only *not* hurt them, but will make them root better. German chamomile is sown (or self-sown) in spring or autumn, and the flower heads picked when in full bloom in summer. Also as noted, the German variety will produce many more flowers per branch than the

CHAMOMILE (ROMAN)

Roman type, so if tea rather than lawn is your destination, that is probably the correct choice. In any case, do plant some, as both are lovely and health-giving plants, dry some flower heads, and render yourself a soothing cup of the most popular herbal infusion in existence.

❧ 13. Chervil ❧
Anthriscus cerefolium

"Cherville . . . with other Herbs are never to be wanting in our
Sallets . . . being exceedingly wholesome and chearing to the Spirits."

—John Evelyn, *Acetaria: A Discourse of Sallets,* 1699

Apparently, you have to love a cheerful herb. Native to the crags of southern Russia and the Middle East, and a close cousin to both carrots and parsley, true chervil (*Anthriscus cerefolium*) is not to be confused with either sweet chervil (*Scandix odorata*) or Spanish chervil (*Myrrhis odorata*), also known as sweet cicely, both of which bear a resemblance to it and share its aniselike scent and savor. A basketful of suitably venerable chervil seeds, dating to the fourteenth century B.C., was unearthed from Tutankhamun's tomb, but, oddly, there is negligible mention of chervil in ancient Egypt. It was the Romans who first carried chervil into Europe, ultimately delivering it into France in about the first or second century A.D., where it found a happy, mainly culinary home. Interestingly, chervils (although this reference is clearly originally linked to Spanish chervil) were once collectively referred to as *myrrhis,* as the scent of their volatile oil was thought to resemble that of the resinous *myrrh* so famously delivered to the Christ Child by Caspar, king of Tarsus, on Christmas Eve. Because of this olfactory connection, chervil became closely associated with Easter and the Resurrection, and it is still traditional in many countries to serve chervil soup on Maundy Thursday in commemoration of the Last Supper.

Pliny the Elder commented in the first century A.D. that "chervil was a fine herb to comfort the cold stomach of the aged," and Nicholas Culpeper similarly reports in the seventeenth century that "the garden chervil doth moderately warm the stomach . . . it is good to provoke urine, or expel the stone in the kidneys, to send down women's courses and to help the pleurisy and prickling of the sides." John Gerard, somewhat less enthusiastic, warns in the same century that chervil ". . . has a

CHERVIL

certain windiness, by meanes whereof it provoketh lust." The *"chearing"* property noted by John Evelyn was also a common herbal assertion, folk medicants throughout Europe maintaining that a cup of chervil tea would bestow good humor, sharpened wit, and even youth upon the lucky consumer. We know now that the active constituents of chervil include bioflavonoids, which aid the body in the absorption of vitamin C; and, for the most part, modern herbal medicine concurs: chervil is a "warming herb" that can help stimulate the appetite, act as a mild diuretic, and aid in digestion.

There are two main types of true chervil: plain and curly, both being hardy annuals, featuring lacy parsley or carrot-top-like leaves, pretty, small, white, parsley-like umbels, and growing to about 2 feet. Chervil both grows and goes to seed quickly, especially in hot weather, and, unlike most herbs, will prefer a cool shady spot in your garden as well as regular watering. Additionally, chervil does not take well to transplanting, so seed in place, thinning plants to about 10 inches apart. Chervil matures in about 6 weeks, so succession planting will be of the essence, and keeping the leaves pinched back to prevent flowering and seeding will not only promote bushier growth but will also help retard the "going to seed" idea. Chervil has a famously subtle but immensely refreshing flavor that hints of licorice, is an essential ingredient in the classic French *aux fines herbes*, and is the herbal component that gives *sauce Bernaise* its distinctive savor. However, chervil's flavor is lost easily, so employ fresh rather than dried and add only at the end of cooking. Here, however, I will pause to recommend an ancient herbal treat: brew a chervil tea by pouring a cup of boiling water over a tablespoon of fresh, chopped herb, let it steep covered for 20 minutes, cool, moisten 2 cotton balls with a bit of it, and place over tired eyes for 10 minutes—infinitely refreshing.

❦ 14. Chives ❦
Allium schoenoprasum

*"I confess I had not added these had it not been for a country gentle-
man, who by a letter certified to me that amongst other herbs I had
left these out."*

—Nicholas Culpeper, *Culpeper's Complete Herbal*, 1653

Despite Culpeper's somewhat pouty inclusion of chives in his *Complete Herbal* of 1653, I personally cannot think of a tastier culinary herb that provides such a blissfully pleasing and care-free show. Members of the *Allium* family, along with garlic, onions, leeks, and shallots, chives are the smallest species of onion and the only *Allium* native to both the New and Old worlds, growing wild across most of the northern hemisphere, from Greece to the south of Sweden on the European continent, in Siberia as far east as Kamchatka, and broadly in North America. Chive cultivation in China dates back to a possible 3000 B.C., with Traditional Chinese Medicine anciently recommending raw chives as an antidote for poison, and chives have been cultured in Europe since at least the Middle Ages, with many attributing their introduction there to Marco Polo. The species name *schoenoprasum* derives from the Greek *skhoinos*, "sedge," and *prason*, "onion," which, in Latin, translates to "Rush-Leek." This onion cultivar's common name comes to us from the French *cive*, which derives from the Latin *cepa*, "onion."

While, in ancient Rome, it was believed that chives could relieve the pain of both sunburn and a sore throat, increase blood pressure, and act as a diuretic, they were not without their naysayers, the clearly wary Culpeper further asserting: "If they be eaten raw . . . they send up very hurtful vapours to the brain, causing troublesome sleep and spoiling the eyesight . . ." Therefore, chiefly valued as a *sallet* herb (as in William Browne's seventeenth-century *Britannia's Pastorals* in reference to the ingredients in Oberon's feast), even this usage was met with some suspicion,

CHIVES

William Rhind reporting in his *A History of the Vegetable Kingdom* of 1842 that "... they seldom find a place in the garden of the English peasant, who, partly from ignorance, and partly from prejudices, does not live much upon these soups and savoury dishes ..." In truth, the medicinal properties of chives, which contain allyl sulfides and alkyl sulfoxides, as well as healthy doses of vitamins A and C and calcium, are similar to those of garlic but proportionally weaker. Therefore, while not wildly efficacious, chives can certainly have a beneficial effect on the circulatory system and in lowering blood pressure, as well as serving as an antibiotic, due to their load of sulfurous compounds.

As noted, chives, with their tasty green stalks growing as elegantly as a decorative grass and topped with those heavenly purple or white "pompoms" of edible flower heads, are exceptionally decorative, particularly as a border plant for a vegetable or herb garden, functioning both as an ornamental edging as well as an opportune pest barrier. Additionally, chives are positively lamblike to cultivate—perennial, hardy to USDA zone 3, and uncomplaining in sun to part shade and almost any soil: despite Culpeper's cranky reservations, what's not to like? Chives can easily be grown from seed, but the best way to increase your holdings is to divide and conquer: just dig up a clump, tease the bulblets into several smaller clumps, and replant. Cut back chives after flowering to about 2 inches above ground, and they will reward you with new growth and another pretty flurry of flowers as easily as a cut-and-come-again lettuce. In his 1806 book, *Attempt at a Flora,* Anders Retzius, the nineteenth-century Swedish anthropologist, describes how chives were broadly used in Sweden to add a green bite to pancakes, soups, and fish. I recommend chopping a bunch into a confetti, then sprinkling liberally over mashed potatoes, classic vichyssoise, or whipping into an omelet batter, and freezing the rest (they remain wonderfully fresh-tasting) to thaw at a later date when some summery "green" addition is all you crave.

❧ 15. Cilantro (Coriander) ❧
Coriandrum sativum

"And the house of Israel called the name thereof Manna: and it was like coriander seed, white; and the taste of it was like wafers made with honey."

—Exodus 16:31

C all out the botanical psychoanalysts, as this is a clear case of horticultural identity crisis. In this "two faces of herb" scenario, "cilantro" and "coriander" are the personas in question—but they are one and the same plant. Another lacy, prettily umbled member of the greater carrot family, properly, the plant and "seeds" (actually the fruit) of *Coriandrum sativum* should be identified as "coriander," while the leaves alone constitute what we know as "cilantro." Among other odd truths dancing attendance to this dual-personalitied food plant is the fact that it is not native to those countries most famous for its culinary employment: although cilantro figures famously in the regional cooking of Mexico and South America, it is actually native to southwest Asia and the Mediterranean, and was only introduced into the Americas by the Spanish *conquistadores* in the sixteenth century. On its native turf, however, *Coriandrum sativum* was anciently cultivated by a host of notable early civilizations, remains having been excavated from the Pre-Pottery Neolithic B level (9600–8000 B.C.) of the Nahal Hemel Cave in Israel, an Early Bronze Age site (3500–2000 B.C.) at Sitagroi in Macedonia, and the tomb of Tutankhamun (1324 B.C.) in Egypt. Additionally, it is one of the bitter herbs ordained by Jewish tradition to be eaten at the Passover feast.

Also odd, considering cilantro's controversial scent ("coriander" coming to us from the Greek *koris*, signifying "bedbug," as the unripened seeds and leaves were thought to be fragrantly similar to that unpopular nocturnal companion), is a fourteenth-century-B.C. tablet recovered from Pylos in Greece, which notes that the plant was cultivated there for

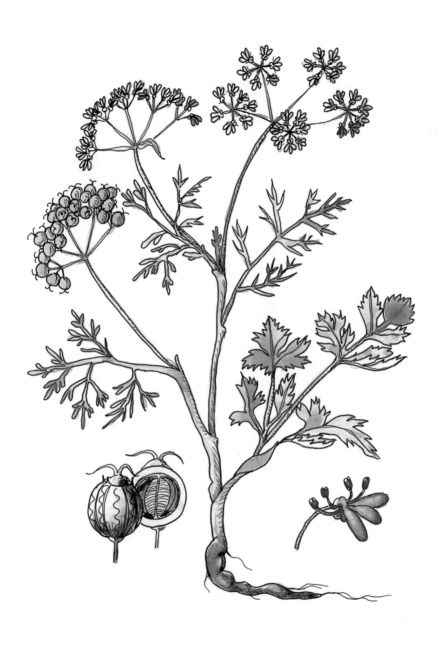

CILANTRO (CORIANDER)

the manufacture of perfume. On the same odd note, *Coriandrum sativum* was reportedly introduced into northern Europe by the Romans for its ability to make spoiled meat palatable by masking the rotting aroma of the *viande* in question with its own pungent bouquet, and, by Tudor times, it was popularly employed in the manufacture of a highly spiced wedding beverage known as *Hippocras*.

Herbally, it was mainly coriander "seeds" rather than cilantro leaves that found widespread medicinal employment, the Egyptians, Greeks, and Chinese all believing coriander had important aphrodisiacal properties. On a less than parallel track, Arab women still chew coriander seeds to ease labor pains. The ancient Egyptians also brewed *Coriandrum sativum* tea to treat urinary tract infections and headaches, and employed the crushed seeds and leaves in poultices to relieve the symptoms of rheumatism. Still other early physicians recommended ingesting coriander to combat flatulence and aid in digestion, and Hippocrates touted it as an effective "aromatic stimulant." As we have noted, many antique herbs brewed into soothing teas and tisanes were recommended for stomach and digestive ailments, and *Coriandrum sativum* is no exception. As well, current research has revealed that the essential oils of cilantro leaves contain antibacterial properties and are effective in cleansing wounds and as a fungicide.

An easy-to-culture annual, *Coriandrum sativum* does not take well to transplanting, so sow seeds *in situ* in a well-lit position in your garden when weather has warmed up (remember: this is a Mediterranean native), ultimately thinning to about 4 inches apart. The only slight downside to this piquant food plant is that it is prone to going to seed, which is happy news if it is coriander you are after and slightly tiresome if it is the cilantro leaves you cherish. In any case, sow every 3 weeks or so and you should be nicely supplied with both all summer long. Harvesting leaves should be fairly apparent. Harvest coriander "seeds" by cutting the stalks after they have fruited, bundling and then drying upside down in a paper bag. Give the bag a few brisk shakes to separate seeds from chaff.

Coriander seeds are generally toasted before use to bring out their spicy, citruslike flavor, and are wonderful combined with cumin and cardamom in Far East Indian cuisine. Cilantro, of course, is what makes guacamole sing, but let us deal briefly here with this controversial cilantro fragrance thing. To put it bluntly, it appears you either love it or hate it, those on the naysaying seat of the seesaw citing an unpleasant "soapy" or "rank" taste and smell. Oddly (yes: one more *Coriandrum sativum* oddity to ponder), some believe it may be a genetically produced enzyme that is responsible for negatively altering the perceived savor of this herb. However, for those of you that are with me, it would be unkind to recommend anything but a classic guacamole here. Therefore, coarsely mash two ripe avocados with a handful each of chopped tomato, onion, and cilantro, a diced jalapeño, the juice of a lime, and a good pinch each of salt and black pepper. Grab a tortilla chip and bully your way to the front of the line.

🎄 16. Clary Sage 🎄
Salvia sclarea

"Some brewers of Ale and Beere doe put it into their drinke to make it more heady, fit to please drunkards, who thereby, according to their several dispositions, become either dead drunke, or foolish drunke, or madde drunke."

—Matthias de Lobel (1538–1616)

Also known anciently as "Clear Eye," "See Bright," and "*Toute-Bonne*," *Salvia sclarea* is native to Syria, Italy, southern France, and Switzerland, the English "clary" originating from the Latin *clarus*, or "clear," referring to this herb's antique employment both as an eyewash and as a means of extricating foreign particles from the eye, Nicholas Culpeper noting in his *Herbal* of 1653: "The seed put into the eyes clears them from motes and such like things gotten within the lids to offend them . . ." As you might expect, "Clear Eye" and "See Bright" also refer to this herbal practice, "Clear Eye" also being a transparent bastardization of "clary." The French *Toute-Bonne* ("All Good") identifies the *Salvia* family's legendary panacea-like reputation, wild English clary (*Salvia verbenaca*) in particular being so esteemed in the Middle Ages that it was referred to as *Oculus Christi*, "the eye of Christ," for its nearly miraculous ability to cure ocular maladies. The family name *Salvia*, of course, derives from the Latin verb *salvere*, "to heal" or "to save," and both the ancient Greeks and Romans believed sages were so efficacious for all manner of ailments that they could literally prolong life.

According to Ernst Moritz Ludwig Ettmüller, the nineteenth-century German philologist, clary sage was first broadly employed as an additive to Rhine wine to give it the savor of the more highly regarded muscatel, and it is still called *Muskatellersalbei* (muscatel sage) in Germany. Clary sage also famously figured in the production of beer as a substitute for hops, lending to it the considerable intoxicating properties so baldly observed by the sixteenth-century namesake of the genus *Lobelia*, French botanist Matthias de Lobel. Unfortunately, the effect of "insane exhilaration" was commonly followed by a really nasty headache, which must have ultimately put a damper on all that "madde drunk" fun. However, clary's most common usage was of an herbal/medicinal nature, in which, aside from its eye-brightening qualities, it was touted for a host of beneficent qualities, including digestive, sedative, tonic, antiseptic, antidepressant, and aphrodisiac. Although no longer an herbal plant of renown, clary's essential oil is still recommended by modern herbalists to help reduce stress and tension, while also having stimulating and revitalizing properties.

Let us, however, stop here to laud the visual merits of this handsome garden denizen. Long terminal spikes of lilac, pale blue, pink, or white, lipped blossoms, similar to garden sage, are held in loose whorls on the tops of stems, which rise from lush rosettes of large oblong leaves covered with a down of fine silver white hairs, the whole plant growing to a stately 2 or 3 feet tall. Planted in full sun, this is certainly a perfect specimen for a soft pastel-hued border, or would be lovely left to self-seed in a meadowlike environment. That said, clary is a biennial plant hardy only to USDA zone 6, so, unfortunately, those of you in cooler zones will just have to forgo this one. Seedlings started in spring will produce a rosette of leaves in the first season but will only flower the following year, usually from June to July, after which, following the ripening of seeds, the plant will die off. However, clary happily self-sows, so there should be cheerful volunteers appearing the following spring in near perpetuity to bloom the year after. Those legendary herbalists Culpeper and Parkinson were both partial to clary leaf fritters, so I will supply you with Culpeper's recipe here: "the fresh leaves, fried in butter, first dipped in a batter of flour, egges, and a little milke, serve as a dish to the table that is not unpleasant to any and exceedingly profitable."

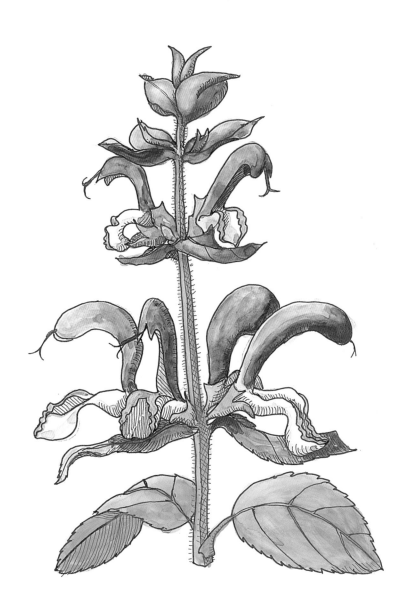

CLARY SAGE

COMFREY (RUSSIAN)

❧ 17. Comfrey (Russian) ❧
Symphytum x *uplandicum*

*"To what purpose do you superadde vinegar to the root of Comfrey . . .
or suchlike balefull additaments, while God hat compos'd this simple
sufficient to cure the fracture of the bones?"*

—Paracelsus (1493–1541 A.D.)

Comfrey is an herbal plant that, while steeped in a notable history of medicinal application, has gone out of favor almost entirely. Its botanical name *Symphytum* derives from the Greek *symphyo*, "to make grow together," and, similarly, the common name, "comfrey," originates in a manhandling of the Latin *confirmare*, "to strengthen together." The folk names of "Boneset" and "Knitbone" should make both of these designations clear indeed as, for millennia, comfrey was cultivated to heal wounds and, most especially, broken bones. Physicians and herbalists from the Greeks Nicander and Dioscorides, second-century-B.C. author of the *Alexiphar-mica* and first-century-A.D. author of the *Materia Medica* respectively, to the Roman Pliny the Elder, author of the first-century-A.D. *Naturalis Historia*, and the seventeenth-century English herbalists Culpeper and Parkinson, all extolled comfrey's considerable healing virtues, Culpeper reporting its curative powers thusly: "The roots being outwardly applied, help fresh wounds or cuts immediately, being bruised and layed thereto: and is special good for ruptured and broken bones . . ."

Mainly, it was the gummy, turniplike comfrey root that was employed, mashed into poultices, and, when spread on muslin and wrapped around a broken bone, actually stiffened into a serviceable cast. Happily, modern research bears out these early herbal assertions: the allantoin-rich comfrey root beneficially effects cell multiplication, and wounds, burns, and bone ailments will, in fact, heal faster with its external application.

Internally, Nicander also lauds comfrey as a remedy for poisons, Dioscorides for gastrointestinal problems, Parkinson to reduce fever, and Culpeper for "all inward hurts, bruises, wounds, and ulcers of the lungs . . ." By the nineteenth century, a cup of comforting comfrey tea was a health-giving staple in nearly every home, comfrey baths became the rage as they were thought to "repair the hymen" and thus "restore virginity" to those in need of such a thing, and comfrey had become the mineral and vitamin-rich fodder *du jour* for livestock herds. And here, my friends, is where we run headlong into a rather brutal fact. Modern studies have proven that comfrey contains pyrrolizidine alkaloids (PAs), which can lead to veno-occlusive disease (VOD), liver failure, and even death. With this knowledge, in 2001 the USDA issued a warning against its internal usage. Therefore, ma'am, put down that crumpet and step away from the teacup.

There are three main types of comfrey: common comfrey (*Symphytum officinale*), native to Europe, central Asia, and western Siberia; "Prickly" comfrey (*Symphytum asperrimum*), a Russian native; and "Quaker," "Russian," or "Blue" comfrey (*Symphytum* x *uplandicum*), a spontaneous hybrid of common and "Prickly" comfrey, native to the Caucasus. Here I will commend to you the 'Bocking 14' cultivar of Russian comfrey, developed in the middle of the last century in Bocking, England, as it will grow only (although easily) from root or crown division and, therefore, is not prone to the invasive seeding qualities of its parents. An attractive, low, dense perennial shrub growing from 3 to 5 feet, Russian comfrey's leaves are large, coarse, and hairy, and its pretty, tubular, drooping, boragelike flowers are generally blue. Rather than a recipe, which I would be ill-advised to recommend, I will close this chapter by relating a tale told by W. T. Fernie in his *Herbal Simples* of 1914, concerning a locksmith whose broken finger "was grinding and grunching so sadly . . . that sometimes he felt quite wrong in his head." When he finally sought the advice of a doctor, the doctor replied: "You see that comfrey growing there? Take a piece of its root, and champ it, and put it about your finger and wrap it up.' The man did so, and in four days, his finger was well."

❦ 18. Costmary ❦
Tanacetum (Chrysanthemum) balsamita

"The balm and mint to make up
My chaplet and for trial
Costmary that so likes the cup
And next it penny-royal."

—Michael Drayton, *Muses' Elyzium*, 1630

Costmary, a member of the daisy family, and also known as "Bible Leaf," "Alecost," and, in France, "*Herbe Sainte Marie*," is originally native to Asia and was introduced into Europe in the sixteenth century. "Costmary" finds its root in the Latin *costus*, signifying "Oriental Plant," with the addition of "Mary," as this plant was historically associated with the Virgin, thus the French "*Herbe Sainte Marie*." "Bible Leaf" derives from the early New World employment of costmary's silvery, dried leaves as bookmarks, primarily in bibles and hymnals as, in part, costmary's strong balsamic fragrance prevented silverfish from consuming them. As well, during lengthy sermons, snoozy Christians would avoid incipient coma by inhaling the stirring scent of their costmary leaf bookmark, or even chewing upon it. As referenced in Michael Drayton's seventeenth-century poem, costmary was also widely used to add tang to ales and beers, Gervase Markham, importer of the first Arabian horse into England, commenting in his *The Countrie Farmer* of 1616 that "both Costmarie" and avens (*Geum*) "give this savour."

Although costmary was used to add a signature lemony/minty savor to foods and beverages, it was cultivated mainly as an herbal plant and seemed to grow in Europe with near ubiquity, the blasé Culpeper reporting: "This is so frequently known to be an inhabitant in almost every garden that I suppose it is needless to write a description thereof." Costmary, being one of the strongest-scented herbs, was often employed as a "strewing" herb, to scent linens and bathwater, and prescribed for a typically wide range of complaints, Green's *Universal Herbal* of 1532 recommending "a strong infusion of the leaves to be good in disorders of the stomach and head," and Gerard maintaining in 1636 that "the Conserve made with leaves of Costmaria and sugar doth warm and dry the braine and openeth the stoppings of the same . . ." Culpeper, in 1653, speaks of costmary being "strengthening to the liver and all other inward parts . . . ," and *Salmon's Herbal* of 1710 comments, "The spirituous tincture helps a weak and disaffected liver, strengthens the nerves, head and brain." Mrs. Grieve, in her *A Modern Herbal* of 1931, also reports on an ancient costmary "oyntment" employed for "bruises, dry itches, streins of veins and sinews, scorchings of gunpowder, the shingles, blisters, scabs and vermine."

Costmary, much like chamomile, is a pretty perennial garden plant that will provide you with a carpetlike sweep of silvery, serrated, very fragrant foliage in spring and small, daisylike yellow-and-white flowers in mid to late summer, the whole plant growing to about 3 feet and being hardy to USDA zone 4. Costmary will prefer full sun and a light, dry, but fertile soil, but, frankly, it's as tough a rambler and a roamer as is mint and will grow fairly anywhere you stick it save in full shade, where it will leaf but refuse to bloom. Much as in the past, contemporarily, costmary is used primarily as a scenting idea, the dried leaves being popular in potpourris, bath teas, aromatic astringents, and the like. Although some assert that the flavor of costmary is nearly as bitter as wormwood, others attest that the infant leaves make a lovely fresh garnish for lemonades, teas, cold soups, and fruit salads, and, historically, the fresh leaves, laid in the bottom of a baking pan, were employed to impart a lemony flavor to cakes. However, here I think I will leave you with John Parkinson's educated advice from his *Paradisi in Sole Paradisus Terrestris* of 1629: ". . . the flowers are also tyed up with small bundles of lavender toppes, these being put in the middle of them, to lye upon the toppes of beds, presses, etc., for the sweet sent and savour it casteth."

ॐ

COSTMARY

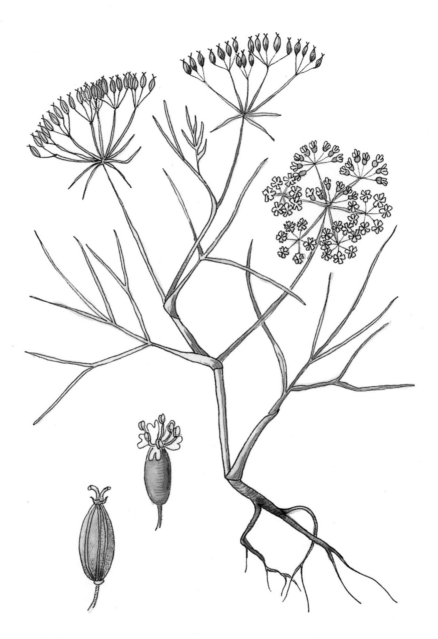

Cumin

❦ 19. Cumin ❦
Cuminum cyminum

*According to Pliny the Elder, cumin was riotously popular with early
Greek and Roman students, as the seeds, when smoked, were found to
lend a romantically studious and, therefore, utterly desirable pallor
to their complexions.*

Another member of the greater *Umbelliferae* family and a cousin to
caraway, parsley, and dill, cumin is anciently native to Egypt,
and has been cultivated in the Middle East, India, China, and the
Mediterranean for 5,000 years or more, seeds excavated at Tell ed-Der in
Syria having been carbon-dated to the second millennium B.C., and others unearthed from tombs in Egypt dating to the sixteenth through
eleventh centuries B.C. Cumin is also mentioned in both the Old and
New Testaments, Isaiah 28:27 reporting on a horticultural note, "For the
fitches are not threshed with a threshing instrument, neither is a cart
wheel turned about upon the cumin . . . ," and Matthew 23:23 reflecting
on cumin's role as a form of currency, "Woe unto you, scribes and
Pharisees, hypocrites! for ye pay tithe of mint and anise and cummin . . ."
The ancient Greeks habitually kept a container of cumin on the table as
we currently keep salt and pepper, and Pliny the Elder described it as "the
best of condiments." "Cumin" derives from the Latin *cuminum*, from the
Persian city of Kerman, where cumin was so broadly cultured that it
gave rise to the ancient Persian expression "carrying cumin to Kerman,"
conveying the same import as the British nineteenth-century adage
involving "coals to Newcastle."

Like many ancient herbs, cumin also attracted a number of symbolic
attachments, although oddly at opposing ends of the emblematic spectrum. It seems the original attachment identified cumin with the negative attributes of greed and arch-frugality, the Roman emperors Marcus
Aurelius and Antoninus Pius, both notable for exceptional avarice, being
given cumin-related nicknames, and misers being commonly identified

as "cumin eaters." This "frugal" or "keeping things close" marker was then moved along the moral track to a more ethically neutral place, in which it was believed that an object could never be stolen or removed if it contained cumin seeds. Then, apparently, this notion of "immovability" was nudged further along the track to the entirely virtuous realm of love and fidelity, and it was customary for ancient wedding-goers to arrive with their pockets loaded with cumin seeds. And, finally, leaping off the tip of the moral rule entirely, in antique Arab tradition, this reputation for "fortifying love" evolved into a popular clamor for a paste made of ground cumin, pepper, and honey, widely prized for its aphrodisiacal qualities.

Herbally, cumin also had a considerable reputation as an antidote for "the flatulency of languid digestion," and, applied as an external poultice, for "the sluggish congestion of indolent parts," both of which I am sure we have all suffered at one time or another. In fact, cumin seeds are a brilliant source of iron, and recent research has shown that cumin may stimulate pancreatic enzymes, promoting digestion and nutrient assimilation, and there is promising research involving cumin's potentially important role as an anticarcinogen and free-radical scavenger. Cumin is an easy-to-culture annual plant growing from 1 or 2 feet tall, with long, lacy, deep green, fennel-like leaves, and equally fennel-like, rose-colored-to-white umbels blooming in June or July, followed by fruiting in late summer (these are the "seeds," resembling caraway seeds). Being a Mediterranean denizen, cumin will crave a long, hot, dry summer, the upside being, of course, that it is also incredibly drought tolerant. With its peppery, nutty, slightly citruslike bite, cumin seed adds famous piquancy to the cuisines of India, Mexico, and the Middle East, and, dried and crushed, is a key component in both chili and curry powder. My mother served this as an absolutely smashing hors d'oeuvre: roughly shred a tin of picked-over crabmeat and toss with mayonnaise enlivened with equal dashes of powdered cumin, cardamom, and coriander. Serve with crackers and to certain social ascendancy.

ॐ

✦ 20. Curry Plant ✦
Helichrysum italicum

"Beef, mutton, rabbit, if you wish,

Lobsters, or prawns, or any kind fish,

Are fit to make a CURRY. 'Tis, when done,

A dish for Emperors to feed upon."

—William Makepeace Thackeray, "Poem to Curry," 1846

The word *curry* is most likely an English bastardization of the Far East Indian *kari,* meaning "soup" or "sauce." However, *cury* is also the more general Old English term for "cookery," derived from the French *cuire,* "to cook," as utilized in *The Forme of Cury,* the gastronomic compendium produced by the 200 chefs in the employ of Britain's King Richard II in 1390, its preface stating with ancient charm: "First it techith a man to make commune pottages and commune meetis for howshold, as they shold be made, craftly and holsomly, Aftirward it techith for to make curious potages and meetes and sotiltees for alle maner of states, bothe hye and lowe." In any case, whatever its derivation, what we know as "curry" has absolutely nothing to do with the curry plant (*Helichrysum italicum*), the erstwhile subject of this chapter, and it is not a plant or even an herb at all, but more a stewlike dish, its earliest known incarnation appearing on Sumerian tablets unearthed in Mesopotamia dating to 1700 B.C.

Indian "curry" as we know it today is really an English Raj idea and is virtually unknown in its current chutney, coconut, and chopped-peanut-topped form in India.

The first known recipe for modern "currey" was offered up by British chef Hannah Glasse in her *Glasse's Art of Cookery* of 1747, and the first commercially available "curry powder" appeared on the culinary scene in 1780. In 1791, Stephana Malcom included a recipe for "Chicken Topperfield plus Currypowder, Chutnies and Mulligatawny soup" in her *In The Lairds Kitchen*, and, by 1861, the unflappable Mrs. Beeton included no less than 14 curry recipes, including "Dr. Kitchener's Recipe for India Curry Powder," in her famous *Book of Household Management*. The standard herbal elements in what we habitually purchase as "curry powder" are turmeric, cumin, cardamom, cayenne, and coriander. Although a few leaves of the curry plant are occasionally recommended to be tucked into the cavity of a fowl to add savor, and the essential oil is sometimes used to soothe burns and rough skin, frankly, it is not really distinguished at either occupation. Therefore, if you wonder why we are turning to it here, you are not without your reasons.

On the positive side, however, the curry plant, a tender perennial plant in the *Asteraceae* family, indigenous to Turkey and the southern Mediterranean, is really a delightful garden plant. Cousin to the strawflower (*Helichrysum orientale*), and, natively, a dweller of dry, rocky slopes, the curry plant is notable for its daisylike golden flowers and soft, truly silvery/gray leaves, similar to those of lavender or, again, some of the *Artemesia*s. Not to be confused with the "curry tree" or "curry leaf" (*Murraya koenigii*), a tropical to subtropical tree native to India, *Helichrysum italicum* is purportedly called "curry plant" because of the strong curry-powder-like fragrance of its leaves, although, in my opinion, their savor is far closer to some of the pungent *Artemesia*s than to "curry." Curry plants are hardy only to USDA zones 8 and above, and will insist on full sun and a warm, arid climate, but are easily cultured annually from seed, so my recommendation is to grow this silvery garden denizen for its comely and fragrant habit but, gastronomically, far better to return to curry's more favored edible identity. Therefore, I leave you with Charles Ranhofer's (nineteenth-century chef of Delmonico's restaurant in London) take on a classic curry powder: ". . . one ounce of coriander seeds, two ounces of cayenne, a quarter ounce of cardamom seeds, one ounce salt, two ounces turmeric, one ounce ginger, half an ounce of mace and a third of an ounce of saffron."

ॐ

CURRY PLANT

DANDELION

❧ 21. Dandelion ❧
Taraxacum officinale

"The dandelions and buttercups
Gild all the lawn; the drowsy bee
Stumbles along the clover tops,
And summer sweetens all to me."

—James Russell Lowell, "Al Fresco," 1868

The dandelion, eons old, and the bane of every lawn fanatic's existence, is most probably original to Asia in our prehistory, although it had naturalized extensively by the time we slithered onto *terra firma*, and was introduced into North America with grave purpose by our earliest settlers as a fantastic source of nutritious sustenance. A member of the *Compositae* family, its closest relations being *Echinacea* and chicory, the dandelion's botanical name derives from the Greek *taraxos*, "disorder," and *akos*, "remedy," signaling a clear panacea-like reputation. In Greek mythology, Hecate, goddess of sorcery, famously fed Theseus, hero of Athens, dandelions for an entire month to bulk him up before his hand-to-hand with the Minotaur, dandelion was included in Chinese pharmacopoeias of the seventh century A.D., lauded by Avicenna, the Persian father of modern medicine, in the eleventh century, and praised in the Welsh *Physicians of Myddfai Herbal* of the thirteenth century, although it did not seem to reach the greater European continent until sometime around 1485.

"Dandelion" originates in the Greek *leontodon*, which permuted into the Old French *dent de lion*, both connoting "lion's tooth," in reference to this food plant's jaggedy-edged leaf form. Folk names for the dandelion truly are dandy, yielding up such tasty morsels as "blow ball," for its signature seedhead, and "piss-a-bed," from the French *pis-en-lit*, for its legendary diuretic qualities. Our old friend Nicholas Culpeper happily recommends it in the seventeenth century as "very effectual for removing obstructions of the liver, gall bladder, and spleen . . . it opens the passages of the urine both in young and old . . . ," adding, however, in typical waspish fashion, after having cited the French and the Dutch for their dandelion enthusiasm: "You see here what virtues this common herb hath . . . and now if you look a little farther, you may see plainly . . . that foreign physicians are not so self-ish as ours are, but more communicative of the virtues of plants to people."

Culpeper was not without his point, as this pesky turf nemesis is not only nature's richest source of cancer-fighting beta-carotene, but also has the highest vitamin A content of any green thing on the planet, while also containing impressive amounts of vitamins D, B, and C, iron, magnesium, potassium, zinc, manganese, copper, and phosphorus, as well as taraxacin, terpenoids, choline, and inulin. All this makes the lowly dandelion about as good as it gets for you: the sap, leaves, and root extracts are all recommended as diuretics, and aid digestion, stimulate bile production, treat liver disorders, and help prevent cancer and high blood pressure, while the root is considered a powerful detoxifier, accelerating the removal of adverse elements from the body. Interestingly, while most diuretics leach potassium from the body, the dandelion leaves a generous amount behind, and the dandelion's milky sap may also be used externally to heal wounds, remove warts, and soothe bee stings.

The dandelion is, needless to say, a tenaciously perennial plant, and there are more than 600 species, our common one identified by its thick, branched taproot, a basal rosette of deeply toothed leaves, and bright yellow flowers held on sap-filled stalks. Each flower head is made up of hundreds of tiny "rays," culminating in that familiar white, globular seedhead so beloved by a pair of pursed lips. Every part of this remarkably nutritious plant is edible (as long as it hasn't been subject to chemical or pesticidal spraying!): the young leaves are exemplary as a salad green and are also lovely sautéed like spinach. The roots are excellent peeled, sliced, blanched, and then sautéed, and the young buds fried in butter are a piquant treat, but my favorite for its moniker alone is "yard squid": cut young dandelion rosettes below the ground with enough of the root to keep the leaves intact, wash well, blanch, dry, dip in a thin egg/milk solution, roll in spiced bread crumbs, and fry. You will never curse your lawn again.

ॐ

❧ 22. Dill ❧
Anethum graveolens

"Trefoil, vervain, John's wort, dill,
Hinder witches of their will."

—Sir Walter Scott, *Guy Mannering*, 1815

Another member of the *Umbelliferae* (parsley) family, and indigenous to the Mediterranean, southern Russia, and western Asia, "dill" comes to us from the Old Norse *dylla*, meaning "to soothe" or "lull," dill being anciently prescribed to quiet colicky babies. Dill remains have been discovered in late Neolithic lakeshore settlements in Switzerland and were unearthed from the Egyptian tomb of Amenhotep II, seventh pharaoh of the eighteenth dynasty. Prescribed as a painkiller in the Ebers Papyrus of about 1550 B.C., dill was also employed by Hippocrates in a decoction for cleansing the mouth, and ancient Greco-Roman soldiers applied the burnt seeds to their wounds to promote healing. In his *Second Eclogue* of about 35 B.C., the poet Virgil speaks of dill as "a pleasant and fragrant plant," and Pliny lauded dill's curative powers in the first century A.D. Intriguingly, dill was a potent ingredient of both benificent wizardry and black witchcraft in the Middle Ages, as noted by the Elizabethan poet Michael Drayton in his *Nimphidia, the Court of Faery* of 1629, when he reports, "The nightshade strews to work him ill, / Therewith her vervain, and her dill." Dill, however was also a common charm *against* witchcraft, as witnessed by Meg Merrilies's incantation over the crib of Henry Bertram in Sir Walter Scott's *Guy Mannering*, and it was also held that, should a witch darken your doorway, the offering of a cup of dill tea would rob her of her ill will.

As early as the eighth century A.D., Charlemagne was serving bowls of dill at his banquet tables so guests who overindulged might benefit from its carminative properties, and this anti-"windinesse" idea was one that has followed dill about for centuries, the anonymously authored British *Banckes' Herbal* of 1525 stating that "dill assuageth wicked winds in the womb [stomach]," and Nicholas Culpeper writing with signature bluntness in 1653, " The decoction of Dill, be it herb or seed . . . is a gallant expeller of wind . . . ," further commenting, "The seed, being roasted or fried . . . dissolves the imposthumes in the fundament," which, I am certain, will make all of us rest more easily tonight.

We know now that dill's health benefits are the product of two components: monoterpenes and flavonoids. One of the monoterpenes, carvone, has a discernable calming effect on the stomach and aids in digestion by relieving intestinal gas. Contemporary German tests also confirm that dill's essential oil relaxes the smooth muscles that control intestinal motility, thus reducing colicky abdominal pain. Additionally, dill's volatile oils qualify it as a "chemo-protective" food that can help neutralize particular types of carcinogens, and dill is an abundant source of calcium, 3 tablespoons of the seed containing as much as a cup of milk.

An annual plant growing to about 30 inches, with signature feathery leaves, handsome yellow umbels, and pungent seed, distinctively aromatic dill is unique in that both its leaves and seeds are used culinarily. Two excellent types are the familiar 'Dukat,' with its tall, sturdy habit and large flower heads, and 'Fernleaf,' a lovely dwarf variety perfect for use as a border plant. Dill loves a well-drained soil and plenty of sun and dislikes transplanting, so sow *in situ*, but it is otherwise a carefree sort, the only glitch being that it bolts easily in the heat and, once it sets seed, will die back in the typical life cycle of annual herbs. Therefore, sow dill spring to midsummer in batches, and keep moist when young, and you will have an ample supply all summer. Both dill leaves and the dried seeds have that unique "dill" savor reminiscent of caraway and fennel: a sprinkling of fresh, chopped dill leaves in a homemade chicken salad or over a plate of sliced, vinegared cucumbers is surely a summer treat not to be missed.

DILL

DOCK (BLOOD-VEINED)

⚜ 23. Dock (Blood-veined) ⚜
⚜ 24. Dock (Yellow) ⚜
Rumex spp.

"Nettle out: Dock in;
Dock remove the Nettle sting!"

—Medieval English cure

According to W. T. Fernie in his *Herbal Simples* of 1914, "dock" is "a noun of multitude, meaning originally a 'bundle of hemp' . . . in early times applied to a wide-spread tribe of broad-leaved wayside weeds." Multitude indeed, as there are over 200 varieties of dock in the vast buckwheat (*Polygonaceae*) family, native or weedily naturalized to the northern parts of most continents, some familiar, and some not so, and many regarded as troublesomely invasive. However, "docks" have been important medicinal and culinary herbs across many cultures since at least 500 B.C., so, noting the most common type in passing, I will pause here to laud the virtues of two of them, one of which you will probably find growing aggressively by your left foot, and one which I will actually urge you to plant in your garden. Numbering both garden rhubarb and the sorrels among its constituents, physically, while having varying leaf forms, sizes, and habits, all *Rumex* possess a signature "noded" stalk habit as well as conspicuously long, thick taproots.

Medicinally, our old friend Nicholas Culpeper had this to say of the docks: "The seed of most kinds . . . doth stay laxes and fluxes of all sorts, and is helpful for those that spit blood. The roots boiled in vinegar helpeth the itch, scabs and breaking out of the skin, if it be bathed therewith. The distilled water of the herb and roots have the same virtue . . ." Modern research has corroborated this internally digestive and externally healing reputation, as both the leaves and roots of most docks are both astringent and purgative, due, in most cases, to their content of tannins and oxalic acid, which chemically provide rumicin (chrysophanic acid), a substance particularly efficacious in chronic skin complaints. Additionally, the young leaves and shoots of many (the sorrels, for instance) were welcome antique potherbs, Culpeper further adding on an intriguing gastronomic note: "All Docks being boiled with meat make it boil the sooner."

As you might suppose, the most common is the common dock (*Rumex obtusifolius*), also known as round-leaved dock and butter dock for the employment of its sizeable rounded leaves as an antique wrapping for butter. Growing to about 3 feet tall with wavy-margined leaves up to 12 inches long, along with the small, green, whorled flower spikes shared by most docks, common dock is a large, brutish, proudly weedy presence in almost every wet-ish place *but* the garden, with leaves so famously coarse that even cattle will refuse to consume them. However, applied as a poultice, they were an invaluable ancient remedy for lesions, wounds, and burns, but perhaps most notably for nettle stings, the verse above being traditionally evoked as the leaf was applied to the spot in question.

Better yet to go out and identify some yellow dock (*R. crispus*), another European import, first described by Linnaeus in 1753, and currently growing abundantly in wet meadows throughout North America and Europe. *Crispus* translates to "curly" for the wavy margin of its leaves, and growing from 1 to 3 feet high with roots up to a foot long and big spear-shaped leaves, *Rumex crispus*, hardy to zone 5, is generally chosen for the various herbal employments for which dock is famous: laxative, tonic, bilious complaints, scurvy, jaundice, scrofula, wounds, and chronic skin diseases. Culinarily, the leaves, stalks, and seeds are all edible, the young leaves raw in salads or cooked like spinach, the flower stalk peeled and eaten raw or boiled, and the seeds roasted and used as "coffee." Additionally, while all docks are vitamin and mineral rich, yellow dock is a true powerhouse, with more vitamin A in its leaves than an equal amount of carrots and more than double the vitamin C of a like portion of spinach, plus a third more protein, iron, calcium, potassium, and beta-carotene.

Blood-veined dock (*Rumex sanguineus*), known more commonly as blood-veined sorrel, is the only variety of dock I will actually urge you to culture in your garden. Native to Eurasia, this is a gorgeous perennial

DOCK (YELLOW)

plant: bright green spear-shaped leaves are ornamented with blood-red veins, making it marvelously decorative in the landscape and, only growing to a foot tall, a perfect choice for a richly variegated front-of-the-border idea. As with other docks, the root is respectably astringent, and the leaves and root offer a valuable cure for assorted skin maladies. Culinarily, the young leaves will add a truly sprightly note (think miniature ruby chard) to salads, and the more mature leaves can be cooked like spinach or made into a warming and nicely astringent sorrel soup or a traditional sorrel sauce to accompany a fowl or roast. However, no matter what variety of dock you encounter (and, for potential herbal employment, this is one I would not hesitate to identify in my precincts as surely there is some not a hop, skip, and jump from you at this very moment), I will leave you with this traditional herbal recipe for the soothing treatment of a whole battery of skin complaints: boil the root in vinegar until softened, mash, cool, mix with lard, and apply. Feel immediate and blessed relief.

25. Elecampane
Inula helenium

"Enula campana reddit praecordia sana."
("Elecampane will the spirits sustain.")

—Ancient Latin verse

Elecampane is thought to be originally native to England, Nicholas Culpeper noting in the seventeenth century that "it groweth in moist grounds and shadowy places . . . almost in every county in this country," although it is now naturalized throughout continental Europe, western Asia, and in the eastern part of the United States from Maine to North Carolina, and westward as far as Missouri. John Gerard reports in 1636: "It took the name *helenium* of Helena [Helen of Troy] . . . who had her hands full of it when Paris stole her away into Phrygia." *Inula* is a corruption of the Latin *Helenium* by way of the Greek *Helenion*, thereby doubling the Hellenic reference in elecampane's current botanical name. "Elecampane" is a corruption of the pre-Linnaean botanical descriptor *Enula campana*, so named for this herbal plant's early ubiquity in the Campania region of Italy. It is also known as "Scabwort" and "Horseheal," "Scabwort" deriving from the ability of a decoction of elecampane to cure sheep of scab, and, according to W. T. Fernie's *Herbal Simples* of 1914, "Horseheal" is a "double blunder": *inula* having been antiquely mistaken for *hinnula*, "a colt," and *Helenium* incorrectly being thought to have something to do with "healing." Therefore, this herb was erroneously if efficaciously taken up by farriers to cure equine hoof and skin conditions.

Never a culinary concept, it was the elecampane root, boiled in infusions and decoctions or dried and powdered, that was antiseptically and astringently employed across many ancient cultures, both externally for skin ailments and internally for coughs, consumption, asthma, and bronchitis. *Inula helenium* was employed by the prophet Job to cure chronic boils, Hippocrates described its effectiveness for maladies and abrasions

ELECAMPANE

of the skin, and Pliny the Elder celebrated its virtues thusly: "Let no day pass without eating some roots of elecampane to help digestion, expel melancholy, and cause mirth." John Gerard reports in the sixteenth century, "It is good for shortnesse of breathe and an old cough, and for such as cannot breathe unless they hold their neckes upright," with Culpeper concurring in the seventeenth century, "The fresh roots . . . are very effectual to . . . relieve cough, shortness of breath and wheezing in the lungs . . . The root boiled . . . is a most excellent remedy for scabs or itch in young or old . . ." Elecampane was also popular as an antique form of sweetmeat and throat lozenge—in 1914, Dr. Fernie explains, "A piece was eaten each night and morning for asthmatical complaints, whilst it was customary when travelling by a river, to suck a bit of the root against poisonous exhalations and bad air." Modern medicine served to catapult elecampane into herbal superstardom with the discovery that its root is the world's richest source of *inulin*, a starchlike substance discovered by the German scientist Valentine Rose in 1804, which breaks down to yield *helenin*, an antiseptic and bactericide so nearly miraculous, an 1885 study demonstrated that a solution of 1 part in 10,000 instantaneously eradicates bacterial organisms, and is particularly destructive to the *tubercle bacillus*. Today, the drug elecampane (*Radix Inulae*) is recommended as a potent internal and external remedy in most national pharmacopoeias.

What is more, elecampane is a strikingly handsome plant, Lady Rosalind Northcote commenting on "the radiant gold of the flowers" in her *Book of Herbs* of 1903, the blossoms being a hefty 3 to 4 inches in diameter and resembling spectacular double sunflowers. These extravagant blooms are held on a stout, deeply furrowed stem rising to 4 or 5 feet from a downy rosette of large (from 1 to 1 1/2 feet long), toothed, ovate leaves, looking much like the leaves of mullein. Best propagated by root division in the autumn, grow this garden stunner in a dampish, semishady spot in your garden both for its physical beauty as well as its herbally important root: a simple decoction for a cold or cough may be contrived by boiling half an ounce of the root in a pint of water for ten minutes. Cool, sip, and survive.

❧ 26. Epazote ❧
Chenopodium ambrosioides

In 1960, modern research into the abortifacient effects of epazote led to the development of the first commercially available birth-control pills.

Occasionally, I have found in the composition of this tome that the identification of herbal divisiveness of opinion can be extremely vexatious, and such is the case with that stalwart of Mexican cuisine, epazote. Native to Central America, South America, and southern Mexico, epazote is an offspring of the near-weedy goose-foot or *Chenopodium* clan (the Greek *chen,* "goose," plus *pous,* "foot,") so named for their common three-lobed leaf shape. The species name *ambrosioides* signifies "ambrosia-like," believed to be a positive reference to epazote's pungent fragrance, which some clearly feel to be fit for a god. Others, however . . . well, let's put it this way: "epazote" derives from the ancient Aztec *Nahuatl* dialect *epatli* for "skunk" and *zotli* for "herb," which is just the tip of this contentious iceberg, although it may go a long way in describing why this herb has never really reached any broad favor outside of its native precincts. Oddly, because some believe cooler climes soften epazote's controversial aroma, the Scandinavian names for *Chenopodium ambrosioides* (in Finnish *saitruunasavikka,* in Swedish *citron-målla,* and in Norwegian *sitronmelde*) all contain a "lemony" reference.

Known by the alternate monikers "Jesuit's Tea," "American Wormseed" (*Chenopodium ambrosioides* var. *anthelminticum*), and *Herba Sancti Maria,* epazote was employed by the ancient Aztecs and Mayans both herbally and culinarily, and was carried into Europe by the return-ing *conquistadores* in the seventeenth century. Chopped, fresh epazote leaves were conspicuously employed as an additive to black beans for their complementary carminative (antiflatulent) effects, but also as an infusion (thus "Jesuit's Tea") to calm an upset stomach. The Catawbas of the Carolinas used a distillation of epazote leaves to treat snakebites and

EPAZOTE

other types of poisonings, while other Native Americans ingested it as a muscle relaxant for coughs and asthma. In the early twentieth century, epazote was widely marketed as *Herba Sancti Maria*, as an expectorant and tonic for asthma sufferers.

However, epazote's most popular herbal employment was and still remains as an "anthelmic": a curative for intestinal worms, including roundworms, hookworms, dwarf tapeworms, and intestinal amoebae, and *Chenopodium ambrosioides* was once listed for this use in the *U.S. Pharmacopoeia*. In a similar vein, there is that interesting subject of epazote research leading to the introduction of the first birth-control pill, mentioned above. Are we beginning to sense a certain pattern here? For this is where we come upon that final hard, hard truth, and the root of all ultimate controversy: a dilution of epazote was popularly employed to kill both worms and human sperm. The truth is, epazote, like some small children and relatives, is lamblike, even beneficent, in small doses but near lethal in large ones, to the point that it can cause dermatitis, vertigo, poisoning, and, in extreme cases, death. And that certainly makes going out for "Mexican and a margarita" a far spicier choice than any of us originally thought.

In reality, this is all a matter of dosage and, in terms of adverse effects, we are discussing the substantially concentrated essential oil here. Therefore, while, today, a synthetic substitute has replaced epazote oil in all medicinal treatments, the amount of fresh, chopped epazote leaf habitually consumed in a Mexican meal or even a lifetime will not only *not* do you in, but will act both digestively and carminatively in the bargain. So if you are an aficionado of Mexican cuisine, my advice? Epazote, *olé*! While clearly only perennial in tropical and subtropical regions, epazote is a carefree-to-culture annual everywhere else, growing from 2 to 4 feet with that signature goosefoot foliage and small green flowers. The taste of a fresh epazote leaf has been likened to a stronger version of anise, fennel, or tarragon, and, as mentioned, is the perfect pairing to a big pot of black beans, so how about whipping up a batch with a nice *pollo con mole verde* tonight?

❦ 27. Fennel ❦
Foeniculum vulgare

*"So Gladiators fierce and rude; mingled it with their daily food
And he who battled and subdued; a wreath of fennel wore . . ."*

—Henry Wadsworth Longfellow, "The Goblet of Life," 1841

Fennel is native to southern Europe and southwestern Asia, although it is currently naturalized throughout northern Europe and much of North America and Australia. A member of the *Apiaceae* family (formerly *Umbelliferae*), "fennel" derives from the Latin *fœniculum*, meaning "small fragrant hay," purportedly for the warm similarity of its scent. In Greek mythology, Prometheus employed a stalk of fennel to steal fire from the gods, this eventually translating to the ancient belief that the gods delivered knowledge to man in the form of a coal carried in a fennel stalk. The Greeks conquered the Persians at Marathon, or "place of fennel," in 407 B.C. and, interestingly, as fennel became increasingly associated with weight loss, the word "Marathon" came to connote "to grow thin." In 812 A.D., Charlemagne declared fennel essential to every garden, it is mentioned in Spanish agricultural documents of 961 A.D., and it was one of the nine herbs held sacred by the Anglo-Saxons, as noted in the *Lacnunga*, a tenth-century medical text, which recommends burning it as an inhalant for respiratory disorders.

It seems fennel attracted a lot of arcane associations during its long history. Besides being associated with weight loss, this stately food plant is aligned with flattery in Clement Robinson's *A Handful of Earthly Delights* of 1584: "Fenel is for flatterers, an evil thing it is sure . . ." We also have the suspiciously unattributed and unsubstantiated proverb, "Sow fennel, sow sorrow." In addition, according to both Gerard and Culpeper in the sixteenth and seventeenth centuries respectively, fennel seemed capable of curing almost anything that ailed you, Gerard noting, "The green leaves . . . or the seed . . . do fill women's breasts with milk . . . swageath the wambling of the stomacke, and breaketh the winde," and

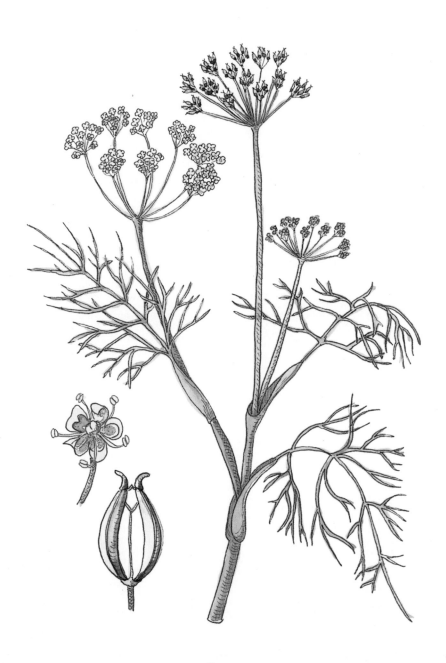

FENNEL

Culpeper lauding fennel's ability ". . . to provoke urine, and ease the pains of the stone . . . stays the hiccough, and takes away the loathings . . . is good for those that are bitten with serpents . . . help to open obstructions of the liver, spleen, and gall . . . ," as well as ". . . shortness of breath and wheezing . . ." In fact, the essential oil of fennel, rich in anethole and other terpenoids, has been proven to inhibit spasms in smooth muscles, contributing to fennel's use as a carminative, and is still included in a few national pharmacopoeias to treat chills and stomach ailments.

And right about here in my research, I was amazed to learn that ingesting even small amounts of undiluted fennel oil can cause nausea and seizures, and those with hepatitis and cirrhosis should avoid it altogether. The bottom line? Much as in the case of epazote, ingesting fennel leaves, stems, bulbs, or seeds is a long trek from consumption of the highly concentrated oil. And, medicinal matters aside, visually and culinarily, fennel is a fantastic edible plant: exquisite of form with as sprightly a taste as dill or anise, whose licorice-like savor it shares, and is surely worth a place in any *potager* or decorative border. I am torn between two cultivars to recommend to you here, so I will briefly laud one that will make a glorious statement at the back of your mixed border, and then another that is sure to be a stunner both in your kitchen garden and on your kitchen table.

Growing to about 5 feet with clouds of feathery leaves and umbels of pretty yellow flowers, regulation-issue fennels are bright green, but the one I will urge you toward here is the gorgeous bronze fennel (*F. vulgare* '*Purpureum*'), every inch of the plant blushed a deep bronzelike purple. Hardy to USDA zone 5 and easily grown as an annual in cooler climes, a tall, billowing stand of bronze fennel in the back of a border is a magnificent sight, and the lacy fronds are famously and superbly utilized in the wrapping or stuffing of a bit of trout or other local catch to impart a subtle aniselike tang. To employ the seeds, leave the central stalk, let the seeds turn brown, and then cut off the whole head and pop it into a brown paper bag to finish (at this point, the entire plant may be cut back to the ground for the season). When the seeds are ripe, shake the bag, remove the seeds, and store, and add liberally to meatloaves and breads, or chew a palmful as a brilliant natural breath freshener.

Florence fennel (*F. vulgare azoricum*), also known as *finocchio*, is a smaller green-fennel type selected for its inflated leaf base, which forms a deliciously edible "bulb." This is an easily grown annual, although even moisture in dry weather and a bit of hilling up when bulbs reach golf ball size to create a blanching environment will not go unrewarded. The bulbs will then more than double in size in 2 or 3 weeks, when they will be perfect to slice thinly with orange segments and dress with a flavorful vinaigrette—or, better yet, roast around a hen with some new potatoes and carrots: cut everything into bite-sized chunks, encircle the hen in the roasting pan, sprinkle with olive oil, chopped garlic and rosemary, and salt and pepper, stir to mix, and roast at 375 degrees for an hour.

❦ 28. Fenugreek ❦
Trigonella foenum-graecum

"Let us sing of Lydia Pinkham
The benefactress of the human race.
She invented a vegetable compound,
And now all papers print her face."

—"The Ballad of Lydia Pinkham,"
early-twentieth-century American folk song

Fenugreek barely squeaked into inclusion in this volume, being herbally almost totally out of favor, its salvation based on an interesting history and a limited contemporary role as a culinary ingredient. A member of the pea (*Fabaceae*) family and native to Lebanon, Syria, southeast Europe, India, and China, "fenugreek" originates in its Latin botanical name *foenum-graecum*, "Greek hay," as it was antiquely employed as cattle fodder and is still grown for herds through parts of Europe and North Africa. Fenugreek seeds carbon-dated to an impressive 4000 B.C. have been excavated from digs at Tell Halal in Iraq, from Bronze Age levels (about 2000 B.C.) at Lachish in ancient Judah, and from the tomb of Tutankhamun (1324 B.C.) in Egypt. Cato the Elder lists fenugreek as an important cattle crop in his *De Agri Cultura* of 160 B.C., the oldest surviving work of Latin prose, and fenugreek was famously one of the useful plants chosen for cultivation by Charlemagne in his Imperial Gardens in about A.D. 820.

Fenugreek saw extensive early herbal employment, the Egyptian Ebers Papyrus of 1550 B.C. recording it in a prescription for burns, Hippocrates viewing it as a "valuable soothing herb" in the fifth century B.C., and Dioscorides claiming it as a remedy for gynecological ailments in the first century A.D. Both Ayurvedic and Chinese Traditional Medicine have employed it for millennia for complaints ranging from the menstrual to the digestive, as well as a general metabolic tonic. Fenugreek was also among the chief ingredients in Lydia Pinkham's Vegetable Compound, a madly popular

FENUGREEK

nineteenth-century U.S. patent medicine recommended for menstrual complaints, and famously featuring a portrait of the stern-mouthed Ms. Pinkham on its label. This humble women's tonic rose to become the subject of sundry bawdy drinking ballads (see above), and observed soaring sales in the 1920s and 1930s for one gloriously simple reason: its availability in a mood-elevating 40-proof version during Prohibition.

As noted, fenugreek has virtually disappeared from the herbal lexicon, William Rhind in his *A History of the Vegetable Kingdom* reporting as early as 1865: "These seeds are not now given as medicine internally, and are only rarely used as fomentations and cataplasms . . . Formerly they were held in more esteem by medical men than they are now." However, modern research has revealed that the seed is a good source of the steroidal saponin diosgenin, used in the manufacture of progesterone, and the chemical trigonelline, which is converted into niacin when the seed is roasted. But, most interestingly, tests have demonstrated significant reductions in total cholesterol, LDL cholesterol, and triglyceride levels in non-insulin-dependent diabetics who consume 25 grams of fenugreek a day. In 1997, Dr. Robert Atkins reported in his book *Dr. Atkins' Vita-Nutrient Solution*: "In very large amounts (between 25 and 100 grams per day), pulverized seeds impressively reduce high blood fats and blood sugar for people with Type I and Type II diabetes."

Fenugreek is a 2-foot-tall annual with light green, oblong, pealike foliage and small white flowers succeeded by this plant's most notable feature: long pointed pods containing numerous yellow-to-brown seeds. In truth, uncooked fenugreek seeds have an unpleasantly bitter taste, which may partially explain fenugreek's descent into herbal obscurity, so the seeds are habitually roasted and ground before use. Powdered fenugreek seed is a favored spice in Indian, North African, and Middle Eastern gastronomy, but seems totally unfamiliar outside of these native habitats. Should you grow some? Unless you are a Type I or II diabetic, not really—buy the powder at your market should you wish to impart a savory Middle Eastern kick to your next *tangine*. If you are, sure. Mix 25 grams of the roasted pestle-and-mortared seed with a spoonful of honey and have a daily down-the-hatch.

❧ 29. Feverfew ❧
❧ 30. Tansy ❧

Tanacetum parthenium
Tanacetum vulgare

When the tansy-lined coffin of Henry Dunster, first president of Harvard University, who died in 1667, was reopened 178 years after his death, the tansy inside was revealed to have nearly perfectly maintained its form and fragrance.

Perennial members of the daisy family and native to the Balkans and Europe, feverfew and tansy are mainly herbal rather than culinary plants of ancient application, and both are still listed in numerous national pharmacopoeias, including our own. However, as modern research has concluded that ingestion of the highly concentrated essential oils of either plant in quantity is potentially deadly, this will constitute yet another example of why "moderation in all things" has its place. So closely related to the chamomiles that the nearly identical feverfew is frequently marketed as such, the chief difference between these family members is that the chamomiles are of a more prostrate habit and it is their flowers that are herbally employed, while the *Tanacetum* branch is of a more erect posture and it is their leaves that are used. These two disarmingly pretty if divisive chamomile cousins were introduced into the New World by the earliest European settlers and, on the North American continent, are now naturalized in drylands and ditches to the point of near weediness from Quebec south to Maryland and west to Ohio.

"Feverfew" (*Tanacetum parthenium*), also antiquely known as "Featherfew" for its feathery leaves and "Flirtwort" for goodness knows what reason, originates in the Latin *febrifugia*, to "drive out fevers." According to Plutarch, *parthenium* derives from the fact that applications of feverfew saved a man's life after he plummeted from the top of the Parthenon as it was being constructed in the fifth century B.C. Tansy

FEVERFEW

TANSY

(*Tanacetum vulgare*), also known as "Golden Buttons," finds its root in the Greek *athanaton*, "immortal," according to Rembert Dodoens, the sixteenth-century Belgian botanist, because of its "everlasting" demeanor or, as Ambrosius Aurelianus, fifth-century leader of Romano-Britain maintained, because it was so effective in preserving the dead. Feverfew, however, also garnered some laurels in the "everlasting" contest, Greek myth holding that the handsomest mortal on earth, Ganymede, was fed feverfew by the clearly smitten Zeus so that he might keep him eternally at his side.

Historically, feverfew was broadly employed as a sedative, abortifacient, laxative, antiflatulent, and popular insecticide, which, I would say, pretty much covers the bases. However, it was as a cure for headaches and emotional malaise that was feverfew's most prominent application, Culpeper commenting, "It is very effectual for all pains in the head . . . as also for . . . sunning or swimming of the head." John Gerard also jumped smartly onto the *mal à la tête* bandwagon: "Feverfew . . . is very good for them that are giddie in the head, or which have the turning called Vertigo . . . Also it is good for such as be melancholike, sad, pensive, and without speech." Modern research has verified feverfew's effectiveness in, if not curing, at least preventing migraine headaches and, in Europe, feverfew currently outsells aspirin as an antimigraine treatment. A 1983 study conducted by the City of London Migraine Clinic reported that more than 70 percent of patients saw a decrease in frequency and severity of attacks by chewing several feverfew leaves a day, and a second study at University Hospital in Nottingham, England, revealed a 24 percent reduction in the number and severity of headaches. The key ingredient here is parthenolide, which slows the release of histamines and prostaglandins, while also helping to prevent fluctuations in serotonin levels.

Culpeper has a positive field day with tansy in his *Herbal* of 1627, commending it for such recognizable complaints as ". . . those who are bruised by falls . . . the griping pains of the bowels . . . for the sciatica and joint-achs . . . to close the lips of green wounds . . . ," but also adding with some obscurity that tansy is helpful ". . . in restringent gargarisms . . . preternatural evacuations . . ." and "to help children that are bursten . . ."

Other herbal employments included expelling worms and, much like its cousin feverfew, in hysterical and nervous afflictions, female complaints and, because of its camphorous scent, as a strewing herb to banish flies. Mrs. Grieve, in her *Modern Herbal* of 1931, sums it up thusly: "In moderate doses, the plant and its essential oil are stomachic and cordial, being anti-flatulent and serving to allay spasms. In large doses, it becomes a violent irritant, and induces venous congestion of the abdominal organs."

Therefore, am I actually advising you to plant either of these? Well, yes and no. First of all, many of you probably have some of at least one growing with some profligacy in your neighborhood wild and, if that is the case, my suggestion is to go out and make its acquaintance so, at the very least, you will be able to point it out with a flourish of your new herbal knowledge. Or, if you have designated an herbal plot on your acreage (something I unhesitantly recommend), these are both charming plants indeed, with lovely, lacy green foliage on erect stems growing to 2 or 3 feet high and producing masses of strongly aromatic clusters of sunny flowers: daisylike, yellow-surrounded-by-white florets in the case of feverfew, and "golden buttons" in the case of tansy. Widely adapted to practically anywhere unsoggy, they seem to adore drought and poor soil, and are hardy to USDA zone 5, if not 4. Sow seeds superficially in a sunny spot, pinch off the growing tips in the first year to encourage leaf growth and a nice bushy habit, and propagate by dividing and transplanting in spring.

And, finally, am I really urging you to employ either of these pretty herbs in some way? Well, yes and no. If I suffered from migraines, would I chew a couple of feverfew leaves a day? You bet. If I had an insect problem, would I hang a fragrantly camphorlike bunch of feverfew or tansy from a convenient tree or rafter to ward them off? Definitely. Would I dry some bunches of tansy to scent the house and provide a bit of sunny color in the doldrums of winter, or simply plant a cloud of feverfew or tansy at the edge of a garden path just so I had the pleasure of its lacy, sunny presence and the chance of fragrantly brushing against it? Try me.

❧ 31. Garden Cress ❧
❧ 32. Watercress ❧
❧ 33. Indian Cress (Nasturtium 'Alaska') ❧

Lepidium sativum

Rorippa nasturtium-aquaticum

Tropaeolum majus 'Alaska'

> *"Of darting fish, that on a summer morn*
>
> *Adown the crystal dykes of Camelot*
>
> *Come slipping o'er their shadows on the sand . . .*
>
> *Betwixt the cressy islets, white in flower."*

—Alfred, Lord Tennyson, "Geraint and Enid," 1859

I have elected to discuss with you not one but three different cresses, each coming to us from an entirely different botanical family and each dwelling in that horticultural shadowland between vegetable and herb, or what John Evelyn, the sixteenth-century English herbalist, would term a *sallet*. Although there are others, the three cresses that will capture our attention here are the common garden cress (*Lepidium sativum*), indigenous to western Asia, watercress (*Rorippa nasturtium-aquaticum*), also known as *Nasturtium officinale* and native to Eurasia, and Indian cress (*Tropaeolum majus*), the familiar and admirably blossomed nasturtium native to Peru (thus "Indian"). All are generally consumed fresh and green and all are prized for two important commonalities, the first being their signature peppery bite, which, historically, was both an affordable and locally culturable alternative to *Piper nigrum*, Philip Miller, founder of the Chelsea Physic Garden, commenting in the *Gardener's Dictionary* of 1768, "the leaves have often been used by the country people to give a relish to their viands instead of Pepper, from whence it had the appellation of Poor Man's Pepper." Also notable is their shared vitamin and nutrient content, historically thought to boost brain power, an ancient Greek proverb urging, "eat cress, and learn more wit."

The Persians and Cypriots seem to be the first to record the culture of garden cress. By 380 A.D. it was listed as a food plant of consequence by Palladius, Roman author of *De Re Rustica*, and, by 800 A.D. it had made its way into Charlemagne's list of useful plants, the *Capitulare de Villis*. It was known by a number of evocative historic sobriquets, including "Peppergrass" for its signature "bite," "Towne" cress, as it was customarily grown in *tonnes* or "enclosures," and *"Passe-rage,"* from the French *passer*, "to drive away," and *rage*, "madness," because of its reputed ability to cure rabies. According to Rhind's *A History of The Vegetable Kingdom* of 1865, garden cress was delivered into England in about 1548, and by the same century, all three varieties, 'Common,' 'Broad Leaf,' and 'Curled,' had been identified. In 1821, William Cobbett writes in his *The American Gardener*: "The curled is the prettiest and is, therefore, generally preferred, but the plain is the best." An annual and easily cultured food plant, *Lepidium sativum* is mainly grown for consumption at seedling stage in *sallets*, when its three-lobed leaves are at their tenderest, although they are still edible at maturity, when the plants will bear tiny white flowers, and, finally, "Shepherd's purse"-like seed pouches. Garden cress is nicely low in calories but pleasingly high in minerals and vitamins, particularly vitamins A, B, C, and E, so sow seeds every two weeks to enjoy a spicy supply all summer.

W. T. Fernie exclaimed in his *Herbal Simples* of 1914, "The Watercress . . . is among Cresses, to use an American simile, the 'finest toad in the puddle.'" Native to Europe and Asia, and a familiar denizen of cool flowing streams and stiller aquatic surfaces, watercress was recommended by Xenophon, the fourth-century-B.C. Greek historian, to be fed to children in order to improve their growth and minds. Xerxes, the Persian king of the same century, commanded its consumption by his soldiers for its health-giving benefits, and watercress was also lauded as a medicinal plant by Dioscorides in 77 A.D., who additionally noted that it was *always* harvested from the wild, with the British garden designer Batty Langley concurring in 1728 in his *New Principles of Gardening* that watercresses "are never cultivated in the garden."

Nicholas Messinger of Erfurt, Germany, is credited with being the

GARDEN CRESS

WATERCRESS

first person to actually grow this peppery food plant, in the middle of the sixteenth century, and, by the turn of the seventeenth century, Sir Francis Bacon, the English father of the "scientific revolution," was opining hopefully: "The eating of watercress doth restore the wanted bloom to the cheeks of old-young ladies." It is reported that a farmer near London began its cultivation in Britain in 1808, but by the end of that century, Eliza James, "The Watercress Queen," who, as a child, hawked watercress around the factories of Birmingham, England, was moving 50 tons of it per weekend. The *Daily Mirror* reported at her death in 1927: "For a woman by her own unaided efforts to have amassed £20,000 three or four times over by selling watercress is surely one of the most wonderful romances of business London has ever known."

Watercress has been considered a purifier of the blood, a tonic, and a general revitalizer since it first extended its fresh greenery above an antediluvian surface, therapeutic employments running the gamut from treating head colds and digestive ailments to combating wrackings of the nervous system, bad complexions (mashed with vinegar and applied), and use as an ascorbutic (scurvy preventative). Nicholas Culpeper snippily informs us in 1653 that "watercresse . . . is a good remedy to cleanse the blood in spring . . . and consumes the gross humours winter has left behind: those that would live in health may use it if they please, if they will not, I cannot help it." Dr. Thomas King Chambers, American author of the *Manual of Diet in Health and Disease* of 1875, earnestly attests: "I feel sure that the infertility, pallor, foetid breathe, and bad teeth . . . of our town populations are to a great extent due to their inability to get fresh ascorbutic vegetables . . . therefore I regard the Watercress seller as one of the saviours of her country."

Watercress, in fact, is an excellent source of vitamins A, C, and K, potassium, iodine, iron, copper, and calcium, and its chlorophyll-rich leaves are currently being touted as an effective neutralizer of free radicals, making it powerfully antioxidant. Therefore, as it is currently naturalized through much of the United States, if you have a gently running stream near you, go find some watercress, dig up wads of it, and pop them into your local muck—otherwise, go purchase some at your local market and compose a classic watercress sandwich to gobble at tea time: process a stick of butter with a handful of chopped watercress, a squeeze of lemon, and some grindings of black pepper, slather on crustless rounds of thin white bread, add a fresh sprig of watercress to each, and top with another slathered round. Pile on a silver salver and dress to impress.

There are two forms of Indian cress, our common nasturtium, *Tropaeolum minus*, the dwarf form, and *T. Majus*, the more familiar larger-leaved and blossomed, climbing variety. *Nasturtium* is the Latin for "cress," coming to us from *nasus*, "nose," and *tortus*, "twisted," in reference to the "nose-twisting" aspect of the cress family's peppery scent. *Tropaeolum*, meaning "trophy," refers to this ornamental creeper's shieldlike leaves and the beautiful spurred blossoms, which were thought to be reminiscent of a warrior's helmet. John Gerard received seeds of the *T. minus* from Paris and lists this "rare and faire" plant in his *Herball* of 1597, and, in 1629, John Parkinson glows: "The likenesse . . . of this flower . . . is of so great beauty and sweetnesse withall, that my Garden of delight cannot bee unfurnished of it." *T. majus* was introduced to France, and then England, from Peru in 1684, and, by the eighteenth century, it was the most prized of all cresses, with Stephen Switzer, leading light of the *ferme ornée* ("ornamental farm") style of British landscape design, writing in his *Practical Kitchen Gardiner* of 1727: "Of the cresses there are three or four sorts that are admitted into the garden . . . the Indian kind is recommended above all."

Indian cress reached North America with the Spanish explorers in the seventeenth century, and by 1793, Virginian John Randolph was noting of this exotic cultivar in his *A Treatise on Gardening*: "It is thought the flower is superior to a radish in flavour, and is eat in salads or without." By 1804, American plantsman Bernard McMahon was enthusing in his *American Gardener*: "Few ornamental plants are better known or more generally cultivated than the Nasturtium." I agree with Parkinson in feeling that a summer garden is nearly incomplete without nasturtiums rambling over a wall, lining a path, or being trained up a topiary form, and I am particularly fond of the variety 'Alaska,' with its variegated leaves and particolored blossoms. As notably ascorbutic and vitamin-rich as its cousin cresses, surely there's a place for a tumble of these in every blossom-filled bower.

ॐ

INDIAN CRESS (NASTURTIUM 'ALASKA')

GARLIC

✣ 34. Garlic ✣
Allium sativum

"Garlic is as good as ten mothers."

—Ancient Telugu proverb

Botanists believe garlic originated in west-central Asia and south-western Siberia, as garlic's wild cousin *Allium longicuspis* grows rampantly near Afghanistan's northern border and in the southern portion of the Ukraine. "Garlic" comes to us from the Old English *gar leac*, meaning "spear leek," and *Allium sativum* derives from the Celtic *allium,* "hot" or "burning," in reference to garlic's pungent personality, and the Latin *sativum,* "cultivated." Archeologists have unearthed clay replicas of garlic bulbs from tomb sites at El Mahasna in Egypt dating to 3700 B.C., and Tutankhamun was sent on to the afterlife accompanied with basketfuls in 1324 B.C. The builders of the pyramids were known to subsist almost exclusively on a diet of raw garlic and onions, the earliest Olympians chewed it to enhance their performance, and the Greek legions so famously consumed it to gird themselves for battle that, planting it wherever they conquered, they ultimately served to spread garlic throughout Europe. Garlic reached the Americas with the first European explorers, Hernándo Cortés reporting to King Charles V in 1520 of "all kinds of green vegetables, especially onions, leeks, garlic" growing at the Aztec capital of Tenochtitlan.

Historically, garlic was recognized as, well . . . perhaps a bit *too* healthy. Both the Greek and Roman aristocracies rejected it outright: in Greece, anyone reeking of garlic was barred from entering a temple, and in Rome it was considered valuable only to increase the stamina of laborers. The prophet Mohammed went further and related that when Satan was cast out of the Garden of Eden, wherever his left foot touched the earth, garlic sprang up, and Horace, the first-century-A.D. Roman lyric poet, identified it as "more poisonous than hemlock." On the other hand, Greek midwives habitually placed a necklace of garlic around a newborn's neck to protect it against ill humors and, in medieval Europe, braids of garlic were hung at the entrance of homes to ensure that evil and disease would not enter. On a slight aphrodisiacal detour, Palestinian tradition held that if a bridegroom wore a clove of garlic in his buttonhole, he would be assured a successful wedding night (feel free to try this one on your next date, but I will not be responsible for the consequences).

The Egyptian Ebers Papyrus of 1550 B.C. recommends garlic for 22 different ailments, the second-century B.C. Sanskrit *Charaka Samhita* applauds it for heart disease, rheumatism, digestive upsets, epilepsy, and leprosy, and the Talmud touts it as a sexual aid, urging men to eat garlic on Friday to prepare them for lovemaking on the Sabbath, when a bout of sheet-tossing was religiously encouraged. Hippocrates lauded it as both laxative and diuretic, and Aristotle as a cure for rabies. Garlic was one of 365 known plants cultivated medicinally in the Far East by 200 B.C., Pliny the Elder suggested it for 61 separate maladies in the first century A.D., and in the second century A.D. the Greek physician Galen dubbed it the "heal-all" of the people. In 1858, it was none other than Louis Pasteur who ultimately proved garlic to be a supremely efficacious bactericide, a single milligram of raw garlic juice proving to be as effective as 60 milligrams of penicillin.

Garlic's antibiotic effect is attributed to its alliin content, the sulfur-containing amino acid responsible for the manufacture of allicin, which is capable of eradicating 23 different types of bacteria, including *Salmonella* and *Staphylococcus*. British doctors characteristically applied a dilution of raw garlic to infected wounds during World War I, and Russian army physicians employed the same technique in World War II. Additionally, garlic contains healthy doses of vitamins A, B, and C, and garlic's sulfur compounds help to regulate blood sugar, detoxify the liver, and stimulate blood circulation and the nervous system. Heated garlic renders the compound diallyldisulphide-oxide, which is proven to lower serum cholesterol by preventing clotting in the arteries.

If you have a vegetable garden, you should not hesitate to grow a row or two of garlic, as there are dozens of stellar varieties available, and I urge you to investigate the full wonder of them in your favorite seed and plant catalogue. However, surely the easiest thing to do is to pick up some nice, fresh heads at your local market in early spring, divvy them up into cloves, and plant them upright about an inch deep and 4 inches apart. Harvest when half of the leaves around the base of the resultant bulbs turn brown; braid the rest into a pretty strand of heads to adorn and employ in your kitchen. Once the darling of only deeply Mediterranean, Middle Eastern, and Chinese cuisine, garlic was initially shunned as "overly ethnic" by U.S gastronomes, even flapper-era slang still identifying it as "Bronx Vanilla" and "Italian Perfume." Today, however, Americans consume more than 250 million pounds of garlic a year, so here, despite those early Greco-Roman aristocratic cautions, I will simply recommend a roasted head squeezed onto some crusty French bread as a remarkably healthful bit of kitchen magic fit for pauper *or* patrician: remove the papery outer layer, cut off top of the head to expose the meat of the individual cloves, slather with olive oil, and bake at 400 degrees for half an hour.

❧ 35. Good King Henry ❧
Chenopodium bonus-henricus

"Be thou sick or whole, put Mercury in thy Koole."

—Early English proverb

Although I would include it in this volume for the sheer romance of its name alone, Good King Henry, like other relations in the goosefoot family, is really only rescued from common weediness by its long history of employment as a potherb. Native to Europe and, most notably, England, and a citizen of seacoasts, salt marshes, and waste sites, Good King Henry was alternately known historically as "English Mercury," "All Good," "Smearwort," "Fat Hen," "Lincolnshire Spinach," and "Poor Man's Asparagus." "English Mercury" and "All Good" both derive from Good King Henry's curative qualities in digestive ailments and "Smearwort" from its historical application as an ointment for wounds, John Gerard stating in his *Herbal* of 1597, ". . . they do scour and mundify," and early American herbalist Christopher Sauer commenting in his *Herbal Cures* of 1774, "Good King Henry . . . may be laid green on all angry rotten injuries." "Fat Hen" originates in the German *Fette Henne*, as Good King Henry was used there to fatten poultry, and "Lincolnshire Spinach" and "Poor Man's Asparagus" arise from this food plant's popularity as both a potherb and a near-invasively available asparagus substitute, particularly in the Lincolnshire area of Great Britain.

Along with several other closely related plants, Good King Henry was also lumped under the catch-all "blite," from the Greek *bliton*, "insipid," referring to its less-robust-than-spinach flavor. John Evelyn, although commenting in his *Acetaria* of 1699 that the "tops may be eaten as sparagus, or sodden in pottage. . . ," also adds waspishly, "'tis insipid enough." The sixteenth-century Flemish botanist Rembert Dodoens maintained the name "Good King Henry" was given the plant to distinguish it from a similar poisonous one called *Malus Henricus* ("Bad

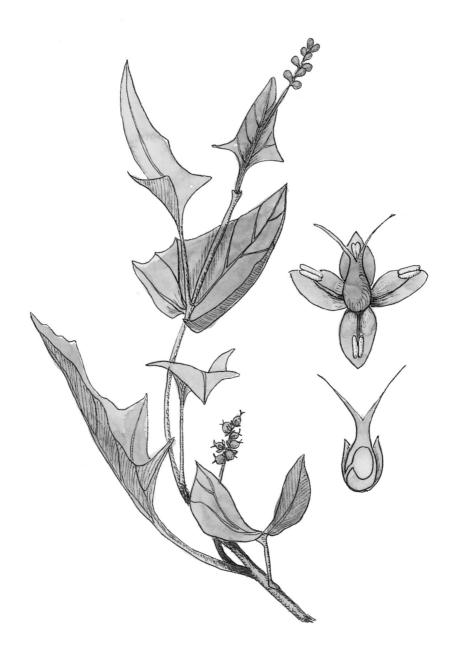

GOOD KING HENRY

Henry"), and Lady Rosalind Northcote reports in her *Book of Herbs* of 1903: "Various writers have tried to attach it to our successive kings of that name, with a want of ingenuousness and ingenuity equally deplorable. Grimm traces it back till he finds it was one of the many plants appropriated to 'Heinz' or 'Heinrich'—the 'household goblin' who plays tricks on the maids, or helps them with their work, and asks no more than a bowl of cream set overnight for his reward. . ." So much for that claim to the crown.

Good King Henry, like most goosefoots, is a healthy spinachlike sort of perennial plant, containing nutritious quantities of iron in the form of digestible organic compounds, and being gently laxative, although, because of its oxalic acid content, people prone to rheumatism, arthritis, or gout should consume this good king only in moderation. Although not exactly a vivaciously attractive plant (read: "somewhat weedy-looking"), Good King Henry rises to about 2 feet on a stout fleshy stem, with large, dark green arrow-shaped leaves and tiny yellowish green flowers held in spikes, and is hardy to USDA zone 6 at least. *Chenopodium bonus-henricus* is best grown from seed as it seems to resist transplanting, William Rhind even going so far as to observe in his *A History of the Vegetable Kingdom* of 1865: "Good King Henry, which makes a very estimable spinach or asparagus in its native country, might make a very sorry one if removed to a place where it is not indigenous." However, given its own semishady plot and once established (during the first year, no picking or cutting), a patch of Good King Henry will be an enviable perennial producer of fresh healthy greens. The young leaves, like those of Good King Henry's goosefoot cousins the orachs, are an excellent spinach substitute, either sautéed in olive oil and garlic *a l'Italienne* or, following the ancient English tradition, "sodden in a pottage" (boiled in broth). However, the real delicacy is the young shoots, harvested in spring when as thick as a pencil, peeled, boiled, lightly buttered, and eaten with a squeeze of lemon as scrumptiously as asparagus.

♉

❧ 36. Horehound ❧
Marrubium vulgare

"Here hore-hound 'gainst the mad dog's ill
By biting, never failing."

—Michael Drayton, *Muses' Elyzium*, 1630

There seem to be a number of theories about how horehound, a *habitué* of dry waste sites in Britain and northern Europe, and weedily naturalized following introduction by the earliest colonists in the United States, got its interesting common sobriquet. Some maintain it derives from the Old English *har hune*, meaning "downy plant," although W. T. Fernie in his *Herbal Simples* of 1914 attributes the meanings of "hoary" (*hara*) and "honey" (*hune*) to those same Anglo-Saxon terms. Still others believe the name comes to us from *Horus*, the Egyptian god of the sky and light, the Egyptians anciently calling the plant the "Seed of Horus." There are two types of horehound, black (*Ballota nigra*) and white (*Marrubium vulgare*), the black variety also known as "Black Stinking Horehound"—so, although credited with the same medicinal applications, it is to the more popular white variety we will wisely cleave in this chapter. The Latin *Marrubium* is said to be derived either from *Maria urbs*, an ancient Roman town, or from the Hebrew *marror*, "bitter juice," many believing horehound to be one of the original bitter herbs of the Passover feast.

Although recommended for a variety of antique maladies, from indigestion and jaundice to earaches, failing eyesight, and even, according to Count Angelo De Gubernatis, the late-nineteenth-century Italian philologist, as a "contre-poison magique," horehound had two principle herbal applications: as a topical poultice for wounds and taken internally as a tincture or infusion, or, most memorably, in the guise of a still-available, commercially produced sugared lozenge, as a remedy for coughs and asthma. In 1597, John Gerard praised horehound thusly: "Syrup made of the greene fresh leaves and sugar is a most singular remedie against the

HOREHOUND

cough and wheezing of the lungs . . . ," and Nicholas Culpeper reiterated in 1653 that it was ". . . an excellent help to evacuate tough phlegm and cold rheum from the lungs of aged persons, especially those who are asthmatic and short winded." Additionally, Gerard counsels it for "those that . . . have been bitten of serpents" and for "mad dogge's biting," and Culpeper addends, "the green leaves bruised, and boiled in hog's-grease into an ointment, heals the bites of dogs," ". . . purge foul ulcers," and ". . . stay running and creeping sores."

Horehound's chief constituent is marrubin, which gives it its legendary expectorant qualities, along with sesquiterpene bitters, tannins, flavonoids, and healthy amounts of vitamins A, B, C, E, and F, iron, potassium, and sulfur. And while the U.S. Food and Drug Administration ultimately deemed horehound "ineffective" for its traditional uses, it has been approved for contemporary treatment of bronchial problems by the German E Commission, this group finding that horehound stimulates discharge of bronchial mucus and is therefore beneficial in the treatment of croup, bronchitis, and whooping cough. As well, the finely chopped leaves, mixed with honey and chewed, have been found to ease sore throats and relieve hoarseness, and a horehound salve is, in fact, useful in the disinfection of wounds.

Horehound is really a very handsome low-growing plant: a minty-looking, bushy thing growing to about 2 feet tall and bearing small, dark green, wrinkled leaves, felty white on the underside, and small white flowers forming dense whorls. It blooms in the second year from June to August on square, hairy stems (thus all the "downy," "hoary" references), and it would make a rather nice front-of-the-border filler plant. However, it being impressively hardy and easily grown from seed or root division, you probably have some growing in a patch of poor dry soil (which it favors) within a lozenge's toss of your front door. Therefore, my advice is, should you be feeling the onslaught of a cold, go out and find some, pluck a handful of leaves, infuse them for 10 minutes in a cup of boiling water, sip, and repeat religiously 3 or 4 times a day.

❧ 37. Horseradish ❧
Armoracia rusticana 'Variegata'

"The radish is worth its weight in lead,
the beet its weight in silver,
the horseradish its weight in gold."

—The Pythia (Delphic oracle)
to Apollo, eighth century B.C.

A member of the *Brassicaceae* family and a cousin to all "cole" crops as well as the mustards, whose hot temperament and essential oil (allyl isothiocyanate) it shares, "horseradish" is believed to be a bastardization of the German *meerrettich* or "sea radish" ("radish" from the Latin *radix* for "root"), as it grew historically by the sea, the *meer* ("sea") then being manhandled to *mahre* ("mare"), thus "mareradish," and, finally, "horseradish." The "horse" idea is also believed to at least partially originate in this brute of a plant's size and "coarseness," and *Armoracia* also identifies a seaside habit: the Latin *ar*, "near," wedded to *mor*, "the sea."

Although originally native to Russia, Hungary, and western Asia, horseradish is one of the ancient bitter herbs celebrated in the Jewish Passover seder. Cato discusses it in his *De Agri Cultura* of the second century B.C., it is most probably the *Amoracia* mentioned by Pliny the Elder for its medicinal virtues in his *Naturalis Historia* of 77 A.D., and, as Delphically declared above, while radishes and beets were re-created in the baser metals of lead and silver as objects of worship, horseradish alone was replicated in gold.

William Turner refers to horseradish as "Redcole" in his *Herbal* of 1551, and, in either guise, horseradish figures in countless medicinal applications through the sixteenth and seventeenth centuries, John Parkinson stating in 1629, "The horseradish is used Physically, very much in Melancolicke, Spleneticke, and Scorbutic diseases." In 1653, Nicholas Culpeper adjured

HORSERADISH

that "the bruised root laid to the part affected with the sciatica, joint-ache, or the hard swellings of the liver and spleen, helps them all . . . ," and John Evelyn commended it as an "antiscorbutic" in 1699. In 1765, the American herbalist Christopher Sauer stated that it was good for ". . . sharp, cutting kidney stones and blockage of the matrix . . . ," and a "few tablespoons" of an aged tincture was helpful for "women who are afflicted with wanness . . ." Dr. Fernie concurs with a number of these estimations in his *Herbal Simples* of 1914, stating, "The fresh root of the horseradish is a powerful stimulant, by reason of its ardent and pungent volatile principle, whether it be taken as a medicament or applied externally to any part of the body . . . The root is expectorant, antiscorbutic and, if taken at all freely, emetic."

Perennial to USDA zones 5 through 9 and easily grown as an annual in other zones, horseradish is a striking plant, and none more so than the variety 'Variegata,' with its massive, dramatically and spontaneously cream-splotched leaves and, of course, nearly gargantuan grate-able taproot. Propagated by division when the root is dug up for consumption in the autumn (or in the spring in some areas), the main root is harvested and then one or two offshoots are replanted to produce next year's crop. Older roots become woody and, while no longer viable for culinary purposes, are still dividable for new plants.

John Gerard observed in 1597 that ". . . the Horse Radish stamped with a little vinegar put thereto, is commonly used among the Germans for sauce to eate fish with and such like meates as we do mustarde . . . ," and it wasn't until the mid-seventeenth century that the British embraced horseradish, although even then it was mainly grown at inn-and-coach station gardens and served in "horseradish ale" (a concoction of horseradish, wormwood, and tansy) as a tonic for weary travelers. However, by the end of the seventeenth century, horseradish had become the consummate condiment to accompany an oyster or a classic roast beef among all Englishmen. If you have never had your own fresh-grated horseradish, you are in for a treat, and 'Variegata' will give you the additional luster of its striking habit (I have even seen it strutting its glamorously tinted and ruffled foliage in purely decorative borders). Therefore, find a sunny pocket in your garden for this brawny, bihued beauty to excite both eye and palate.

❧ 38. Hyssop ❧
Hyssopus officinalis

"Purge me with hyssop and I shall be clean: wash me, and I shall be whiter than snow."

—Psalms 51:7

A member of the mint (*Lamiaceae*) family and native to southern Europe and the Mediterranean, hyssop, potentially the most historically prominent herb totally unknown to you, has been a symbol of cleansing and purification since the dawn of impure thought. "Hyssop" derives from the Greek or Hebrew *azob* or *ezob*, meaning "Holy Herb," and it was David, slayer of Goliath, who made the above plea following his ill-advised dalliance with Bathsheba, wife of Uriah the Hittite, which resulted in Bathsheba's pregnancy, Uriah's murder, and David's shame. To cleanse a leper's home, Leviticus 14:4 proposed, ". . . two birds alive and clean, and cedar wood, and scarlet, and hyssop . . . ," and Numbers 19:18 advised in the case of a potentially contagious death, ". . . a clean person shall take hyssop and dip it in the water, and sprinkle it upon the tent and upon all the vessels and upon the persons who were there, and upon him that touched a bone or one slain or one dead or a grave." However, hyssop's most important biblical reference surely must be the account from John 19:29 of the moment the Savior cried "I thirst!" from the cross at Golgotha, and the surrounding soldiers, to mock him, "put a sponge full of the sour wine on a hyssop branch and held it to his mouth." Convention, however, seems to be intent on identifying the *azob* of scripture with either hyssop's cousin marjoram (*Origanum maru*) or the caper plant (*Capparis spinosa*), which are known to grow more widely in the Middle East.

Hyssop's signature camphorous scent and, like its close relation horehound, abundance of the active compound marrubin, were at the root of all this purging and purification, and hyssop was habitually strewn over floors and hung from doorways to impart a pleasing fragrance, act as

HYSSOP

a fumigant, and drive away ill spirits. Additionally, hyssop had two other significant herbal employments: again, much like horehound, as an external poultice for wounds and bruises and, internally, as an expectorant, a strong infusion of the leaves and flowering tops being recommended for lung congestion and catarrhal complaints. Hippocrates prescribed hyssop to treat pleurisy in the fourth century B.C., Dioscorides suggested brewing up a tea for ". . . cough, wheezing and shortness of breath . . ." in the first century A.D., and Hildegard of Bingen, the twelfth-century German abbess/herbalist, maintained that hyssop "cleanses the lungs." John Parkinson jumped on the expectorant/poultice bandwagon in 1629, commenting that "hyssop is much used in tisanes and other drinkes, to help expectorate flegme. It is many Countrey peoples medicine for a cut or greene wound being bruised with sugar and applied . . . ," with Nicholas Culpeper vociferously concurring in 1653 that hyssop ". . . is effectual in all cold grief's or diseases of the chest and lungs" and ". . . takes away the blue and black marks that come by strokes, bruises, or falls." Modern herbalists seem to agree: a tisane drunken or a poultice applied will act promptly and as promised.

Additionally, hyssop is a lovely, small, wonderfully fragrant plant, with thin, pointed leaves growing to about 2 feet high. There are three major varieties, identified by their small, usually blue, but also red or white, tubular flowers. Superb as a front-of-the-border or edging plant and hardy to USDA zone 6, hyssop will be appreciative of full sun and a well-drained soil, and will benefit from a spring trimming for optimal beauty, the only slight negative being that hyssop is rather short-lived as a plant, and will need to be renewed every few years. While, culinarily, minty, slightly bitter hyssop leaves may be added to soups and salads, our friend Dr. Fernie states that, herbally, "Hyssop tea is a grateful drink . . . ," so I will leave you with his recipe: "one drachm of the dried herb should be infused in a pint of boiling water, and allowed to become cool. Then a wineglass full is to be given as a dose two or three times a day."

❦ 39. Lavender ❦
Lavandula angustifolia
Lavandula spica

"Then took Mary a pound of ointment of spikenard, very costly; and anointed the feet of Jesus, and wiped his feet with her hair; and the house was filled with the odor of the ointment."

—John 12:3

Fragrant lavender is indigenous to the mountainous regions of the western Mediterranean and has been employed there for millennia, mainly in a cleansing and aromatherapeutic vein. "Lavender" is thought to derive from either the Latin *lavare*, "to wash," or *livendulo*, "livid" or "bluish," in reference to the blossom color. According to W. T. Fernie, the Greeks called it *nardus* after the town of Naardus in Syria, from which they believed it originated, and it was broadly identified as "spikenard," this term marrying *nardus* with the plant's flower "spike." Legend held that the very first lavender plant, carried from the Garden of Eden by Adam and Eve, was originally scentless, and lavender only achieved its signature fragrance when the Virgin laid the swaddling of the infant Savior over a bush of it to dry. In typical early herbal duality, countless other applications aside, lavender was prized both for its calming and aphrodisiacal effects, having been broadly employed to dispel headaches while, at the same time, being strewn about Cleopatra's chambers to entice both Julius Caesar and Mark Antony, and the well-known 1680 English rhyme "Lavender blue, dilly dilly . . ." originally containing the not-so-well-known lyrics, "Whilst you and I, diddle, diddle . . ."

In the first century A.D., Dioscorides recommended lavender for indigestion, headaches, and sore throats, and, externally, for cleansing wounds, and Pliny the Elder for menstrual problems, upset stomachs, kidney disorders, and insect bites. Hildegard of Bingen recommended a

LAVENDER

decoction of lavender as a treatment for migraines and the essential oil for head lice and fleas in the twelfth century. At the turn of the fifteenth century, "Charles the Mad" of France, who famously roamed his palaces howling like a wolf, and was, at times, convinced that he was made of glass, had his seat cushions stuffed with "spikenard." William Rhind, author of *A History of the Vegetable Kingdom* of 1865, believed lavender was introduced into England in 1568. By 1653, Nicholas Culpeper was lauding lavender for ". . . the tremblings and passions of the heart, and faintings and swounings . . . ," and John Parkinson recommended it in 1629 for ". . . bathes, ointment or other things that are used for cold cause . . . all griefes and paines of the head and brain . . . ," and, on a helpful household note, "to perfume linnen, apparell, gloves and leather . . ." (Interestingly, lavender became so identified with the freshening of linens that, in medieval and Renaissance Britain, laundresses were customarily referred to as "lavenders.") Elizabeth I was known to use lavender to treat her migraines at the turn of the seventeenth century; by 1655, during the Great Plague of London, lavender was being hawked on every street corner to be worn on the sleeve as a prophylactic, and Queen Victoria was so enthusiastic about lavender in the nineteenth century that she appointed one Sarah Sprules "Purvey of Lavender Essence to the Queen."

Modern medicine has confirmed lavender's effectiveness in treating stress and headaches, Mrs. Grieve advising in 1931 that "a tea brewed from Lavender tops, made in moderate strength, is excellent to relieve headache from fatigue and exhaustion, giving the same relief as the application of Lavender water to the temples." However, *nota bene*, Mrs. Grieve goes on to comment, "an infusion taken too freely, will . . . cause griping and colic, and Lavender oil in too large doses is a narcotic poison and causes death by convulsions." Clearly, "moderate strength" is of the essence here. As well, lavender was broadly employed as a topical antiseptic for wounds and burns in the trenches of World War I and, again according to Mrs. Grieve, "In France, it is a regular thing for most households to keep a bottle of Essence of Lavender as a domestic remedy against bruises, bites and trivial aches and pains, both external and internal."

Anyone who has ever driven through the lavender fields of England or France is well acquainted with the particular beauty of this plant, the exquisite mainly blue "wands" emerging on long, thin stems from distinctive gray or blue/green foliage. There are a number of lavender types, the two main ones being "English lavender," *Lavendula angustifolia*, and "French Lavender," *Lavendula spica*, the original Mediterranean "spikenard" of old, the principle differences being leaf form, the French variety having larger, more rounded leaves, and quality of fragrance, educated "noses" infinitely preferring the English type. A Mediterranean native, lavender will only truly prosper in a light (read: "sandy") soil in a dry, open, sunlit position. If you can achieve that, plant away in great, fragrant billows, and employ the fresh or dried flowers in everything from teas and cordials to linen rinses, bath soaks, sachets, and potpourris. I'll leave you with this *receipte* from the consistently correct Mrs. Grieve: "Put into a bottle half a pint of spirit of wine and two drachms of oil of lavender. Mix it with rose-water, five ounces, orange-flower water, two ounces, also two drachms of musk and six ounces of distilled water . . . ," resulting in ". . . a pleasant and efficacious cordial and very useful in languor and weakness of the nerves, lowness of spirits, faintings, etc."

ॐ

Lemon Balm 'All Gold'

❦ 40. Lemon Balm 'All Gold' ❦
Melissa officinalis 'Aurea'

"The several chairs of order look you scour
With juice of balm and every precious flower."

—William Shakespeare, *Merry Wives of Windsor*, 1600

In this tome I introduce you to a number of notable lemon-scented herbal presences in the garden, but none so stalwartly age-old and hardily habited as lemon balm, a *Lamiaceae* (mint) family member native to southern Europe and the Mediterranean. Known simply as "balm" antiquely—an abbreviation of "balsam," which originates from the Hebrew *bal smin*, meaning "chief of sweet-smelling oils"—lemon balm is *not* the pined-for "balm in Gilead" referenced in the Bible, which is the true balsam of Judea. However, lemon balm soon managed to acquire both that legendary plant's herbal mantle *and* its title.

Melissa derives from the Greek for "honeybee" (*mel* = "honey"), and Pliny the Elder says of bees and lemon balm, "When they are strayed away, they do find their way home by it." Gerard reiterates in 1597, "The hives of bees being rubbed with the leaves of bawme, causeth the bees to keep together, and causeth others to come with them." At the turn of the sixteenth century, the Swiss physician Paracelsus, father of toxicology, designated a decoction of lemon balm his *elixir vitae*, William Rhind commenting in 1865, " . . . whereby he was to renovate man; and, if he did not bestow upon him absolute immortality, to produce a very close approximation to that state." The *London Dispensary* endorsed the same view in 1696, affirming that an infusion of lemon balm ". . . given every morning, will renew youth, strengthen the brain and relieve languishing nature," and John Evelyn described it in 1699 as ". . . strengthening the memory, and powerfully chasing away melancholy." According to Mrs. Grieve, lemon-balm tea was famously imbibed by both Llewelyn, thirteenth-century prince of Glamorgan, who lived to be 108 years old, and one John Hussey of Sydenham, who lived to be 116. Additionally,

"Carmelite Water," a popular tonic in which lemon balm was combined with lemon peel, nutmeg, and angelica root, was known to have been consumed daily by the famously cosmopolitan sixteenth-century Holy Roman Emperor Charles V.

In 1865, however, William Rhind cuts sharply to the herbal chase in reference to the imbibed *elixir vitae* of Paracelsus: "Such strange conceits of ill-directed minds have . . . long gone by; and balm, stripped of its fancied virtues, is now only employed as an infusion in preparing a cooling drink, or in giving flavor to a weak, factitious wine." That said, externally, lemon balm has had far more enduring support, as Pliny the Elder reports in the first century A.D., "It is of so great virtue that though it be but tied to his sword that hath given the wound it stauncheth the blood," with Gerard concurring, "the juice of Balm glueth together greene wounds." In fact, lemon balm's balsamic oils make it an excellent surgical dressing—these oils are not only antiputrescent but also actually starve wounds of oxygen as their balsamic resins seal them from infection. And, frankly, whatever Rhind's opinion, lemon-balm tea is still a mighty soothing thing.

Lemon balm is clearly identifiable as a mint clan member, with square, branching stems to 2 feet, oval- to heart-shaped jaggedy-edged leaves, and small white or yellowish flowers. There is the general-issue green variety and also a variegated ('Variegata') variety, which, however, is prone to reverting to green in the heat of most of our summers, so here I will direct you to the radiant 'All Gold' or 'Aurea' type, boasting chartreuse leaves and constituting a perfect plant to sparkle up a semishady corner of your vegetable or herb plot, although it will do just as well in full sun. In fact, perennially hardy to USDA zone 4, lemon balm, being a mint, will pretty much survive anywhere, and will spread with some rapaciousness, so a bit of curtailment will be of the essence. Cut back frequently in season to prevent flowering and seeding, and entirely in fall, and, just like mint, your stand will resprout winningly in spring. This is definitely a tea idea: hot or cold, comforting or refreshing—take your pick.

༄

❧ 41. Lemongrass ❧
Cymbopogon citratus
Cymbopogon flexuosus

Contemporary spiritualists advise adding a sprinkling of lemongrass to your tarot bag to "keep your cards attuned," as well as scattering lemongrass around the table before tarot readings.

Lemongrass, a native of India and Sri Lanka and cousin to vetiver (*Vetiveria zizanioides*), citronella (*Cymbopogon nardus*), and palmarosa (*Cymbopogon martini*) in the *Gramineae* family, is a fairly recent star in the global herbal firmament and is still probably best known for its lemony presence in Thai and Vietnamese cuisine and for the utilization of its essential oil in perfumes. There are two basic varieties of lemongrass, the West Indian (*Cymbopogon citratus*) and East Indian (*Cymbopogon flexuosus*) types, the main difference being that the West Indian type alone contains the active analgesic compound myrcene. Lemongrass has had a long history of herbal application in both India and Africa where, known alternately as "Fevergrass," it is traditionally employed in Ayurvedic medicine to combat *jwara* or "fever," sometimes called the "king of diseases" by Ayurvedic medicants. The *Charaka Samhita*, the oldest extant Sanskrit medical treatise, which dates to the third century B.C., claimed that during the evolution of human ailments, fever was the first to come into being, and it was disturbing not only to the body but the mind and soul as well.

In Tanzania and Kenya, an infusion of lemongrass was also taken historically for fevers as well as being employed as a body wash and perfume, and the Zulu were known to use the plant juice for ritual cleansing. Citral, the main chemical constituent of lemongrass's essential oil, is antiviral, antiseptic, and antibacterial, making it a splendid astringent for troublesome complexions, and recent research also suggests that lemongrass oil is highly effective as a sedative, acting on the central nervous system and, applied to the temples or forehead, being especially useful in headache and stress relief. The only caveat here is that essential lemongrass oil is a powerful thing and should be diluted in a nonactive carrier oil before application.

As you might suspect from its name, lemongrass is a tall, graceful, heavenly scented "fountain" of a grassy plant, boasting light green blades growing from 3 to 6 feet and offering both wonderful texture and movement in a bed or border, as well as constituting an elegant upright focal point at the center of a cascading potted planting. Clearly native to tropical climes, lemongrass prefers humidity and warmth and is hardy only to USDA zones 10 and 11, so the rest of us will just have to treat it as an annual or pot it up and drag it inside come winter. Lemongrass is easily propagated by crown division or, if you can find some in the store, try peeling off the outer leaves of the store-bought stalks, standing them upright in a jar of water on a sunny windowsill until they root, and then planting.

Culinarily, it is the pale tubular core, resembling a slim scallion bulb, inside the fibrous outer layers of a lemongrass stalk that is of interest here. To use, cut the stalk to about 6 inches, remove two layers, and then gently bruise it along its length using the side of a large knife or a rolling pin to encourage that citrusy aroma. Slivers of this tender core may then be added to pungent Thai and Vietnamese-style broths and stews, imparting a rich lemon savor, or may be brewed into a delicious fever- and stress-reducing tea. However, due to the popular employment of this flavorful herb by the fragrance industry, let me direct you here to the concoction of a refreshing take on a very useful insect repellant: mix a teaspoonful of lemongrass oil with half as much eucalyptus oil and 1/4 cup vegetable oil. Shake up in a glass bottle and dab on uncovered flesh as needed on a summer night.

☿

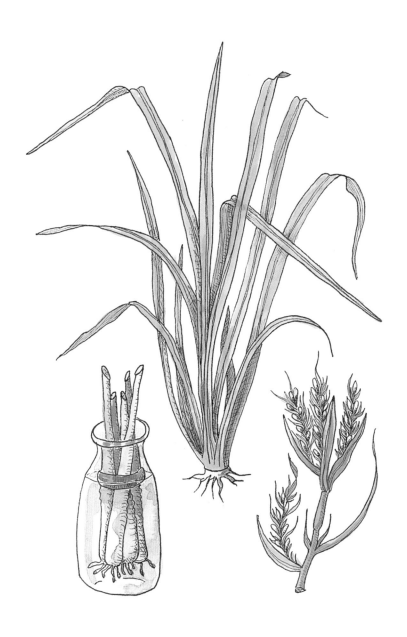

LEMONGRASS

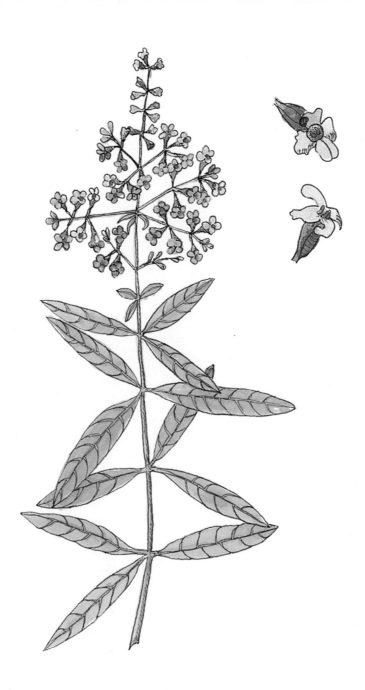

LEMON VERBENA

❧ 42. Lemon Verbena ❧
Aloysia triphylla

Keep an infusion of lemon verbena in a spray bottle in the refrigerator and give your face a spritz at the first sign of the blahs.

I had always imagined that lemon verbena (or *verveine*), with its remarkable citrusy scent, must have a long and distinguished herbal and culinary history. For one thing, "verbena" was the catch-all, early Roman term for "sacred herb," and the *vervaine* of European legend, known by such other evocative names as *"Herba Sacra,"* "Tears of Isis," and "Mercury's Moist Blood," was believed to have been used to stanch the wounds of the Savior on Golgotha hill. In medieval times, amulets of verbena root were habitually worn about the neck to ward off pestilence and witchcraft, and verbena leaves and flowers were employed in countless incantations, evil-dispelling ointments, and erstwhile love potions by aspiring sorcerers. So imagine my surprise when I learned that these near-miraculous achievements belong to another plant and family entirely, *vervaine* or *Verbena officinalis*, and that lemon verbena (*Aloysia triphylla*) or *verveine* is actually a South American plant, native to Argentina, Chile, and Peru, and was not introduced into Europe until the late eighteenth century, when it was imported to Spain for the manufacture of perfume.

Why it was named both "lemon verbena" and *verveine* (versus *vervaine*), when it not only doesn't remotely resemble but also isn't remotely related to *Verbena officinalis*, is a point absolutely no one seems to be able to answer to my satisfaction. We do know, however, that *Aloysia* derives from Maria Louisa—princess of Parma and wife of King Charles IV of Spain, into which country the herb was first delivered—and *triphylla*, from this plant's immensely fragrant whorls of three (*tri*) leaves (*phylla*). This is not to say, however, that lemon verbena did not achieve its own medicinal and culinary reputation once it reached the continent. It was widely touted during the nineteenth and early twentieth centuries as an antispasmodic, antipyretic (fever reducer), carminative, sedative, stomachic, and antimicrobial. Today, lemon verbena is one of the reigning darlings of aromatherapy as its leaves stay fragrant nearly everlastingly, and teas and infusions of the leaves have a broadly "soothing" reputation, lemon verbena's volatile oils and flavonoids being calming to both the stomach and the nerves, helping to reduce fever, and, applied as a skin tonic, serving as a refreshing antibacterial for conditions like acne and boils.

As you might expect, being a South American native, lemon verbena is a tender perennial plant hardy only to USDA zone 8 but may easily be grown as an annual or alternately employed as a potted plant and taken indoors for the winter, although it is somewhat prone to white fly and, being deciduous, may thank you for your trouble by dropping its leaves. Better to buy a plant each spring and watch it grow into a lovely, willowy thing with slender, lanceolate, highly lemon-scented leaves and tiny pale lavender-to-white flowers in the summer, and growing to 3 feet in a single season. Lemon verbena loves sun and warmth and, in zones that don't veer below 27 degrees, you may cut the plant back rather brutally and mulch the crown well, and it should resprout easily in spring. Also, snipping back the growing tips occasionally in season will promote branching and keep your plant nicely dense and bushy. When the leaves are young and tender, chop them into green or fruit salads; older leaves are perfect for an aromatic and immensely comforting cup of tea. Here, however, I will suggest the concoction of a flavorful and healthful *eau-de-vie*: chop half a cup of fresh leaves, add to a jar with 4 cups of vodka, let stand for two weeks, add 2 cups of sugar, shake to dissolve, let stand for another two weeks, strain, and sip when your day has had too many hours.

❧ 43. Licorice ❧
Glycyrrhiza glabra

"She cast her blazing eyes on me
And plucked a licorice leaf;
I was her captive slave and she
My red-haired robber thief."

—John Betjeman, "The Licorice
Fields at Pontefract," 1954

Licorice, native to southeast Europe and southwest Asia, is derived from the sweet root of various species of *Glycyrrhiza*, a genus in the pea family containing about 14 varieties, 10 of them having more or less sweet roots. However, the chief source of global medicinal licorice and the only type included in both the British and American pharmacopoeias is the English licorice, *G. glabra,* toward which we will therefore swivel our binoculars. Indian legend holds that Brahma himself, Hindu god of creation, born in a lotus flower that grew from the navel of Vishnu at the dawn of creation, endorsed the beneficent effects of licorice, and licorice root was one of the 247 compounds included in the Chinese *Wu Shi Er Bing Fang* (Prescriptions for Fifty-two Diseases), written between 1065 and 771 B.C. In the third century B.C., licorice was imported into Greece from Scythia, where Theophrastus reported it grew near Lake Maeotis, and it was Dioscorides who named the plant *Glycyrrhiza,* from the Greek *glukos,* "sweet," and *riza,* "root," in the first century A.D.

"Licorice" derives from this plant's alternate designation, *Liquiritae officinalis,* the Latin *Liquiritia* a corruption of *Glycyrrhiza,* although, in the first century A.D., Scribonius Largus, physician to the Roman emperor Claudius, also refers to licorice as *Radix dulcis,* also translating to "sweet root." Interestingly, the Chinese *gancao* translates to "sweet herb" as well. This sugary tale continues in 1264 A.D., when licorice is included in the Wardrobe Accounts of Henry IV of France, who first coined that age-old political chestnut "a chicken in every pot!" It is described as under cultivation in Italy by Piero de'Crescenzi in his *Ruralia Commoda* of 1305, and John Stow reports in his *Summarie of Englyshe Chronicles* of 1565 that in England "the planting and growing of licorish began about the first year of Queen Elizabeth," most famously in the medicinal gardens of Pontefract (Pomfret) Abbey in Yorkshire, now the epicenter of the English licorice confectionery industry.

Licorice has been recommended as a remedy for sore throats, coughs, and lung complaints across as vast a continuum of cultures and millennia as you could possibly name. In the *Wu Shi Er Bing Fang* it was lauded for wheezing, respiratory illnesses, coughing, and phlegm; Theophrastus found it effective for asthma, dry cough, and pectoral diseases, Pliny recommends it for coughs, John Parkinson ". . . to helpe to digest and expectorate flegme out of the chest and lunge . . . and for all sorts of coughes," and Nicholas Culpeper for "dry cough or hoarseness, wheezing . . . and for all pains of the breasts and the lungs," adding, "The root of this plant is deservedly in great esteem, and can hardly be said to be an improper ingredient in any compositions of whatever intention." We know now that, aside from those signature sugars, saccharose (3 percent) and glucose (3 percent), it is the unique chemical glycyrrhizin (6 to 8 percent) that rivets our attention, stimulating the adrenal gland to produce hormones that dramatically reduce inflammation while increasing immune-important interferon, thereby deflecting attacks to the respiratory system. New research also indicates the immunity-boosting properties of glycyrrhizin show terrific promise in ameliorating other inflammatory conditions like hepatitis, and licorice extract is still a key ingredient in almost all cough syrups.

Licorice plants are graceful things, with feathery pealike foliage, and small pale blue, violet, yellowish white, or purplish flowers, followed by small pods resembling an infant peapod. In the type *glabra*, the pods are smooth, while in other varieties they are hairy or spiny. However, it is what goes on underground that is of chief interest here: to wit, a taproot growing to a depth of a whopping 3 or 4 feet, and horizontal "stolons" thrown off from the root, which can also attain many feet in length. It is

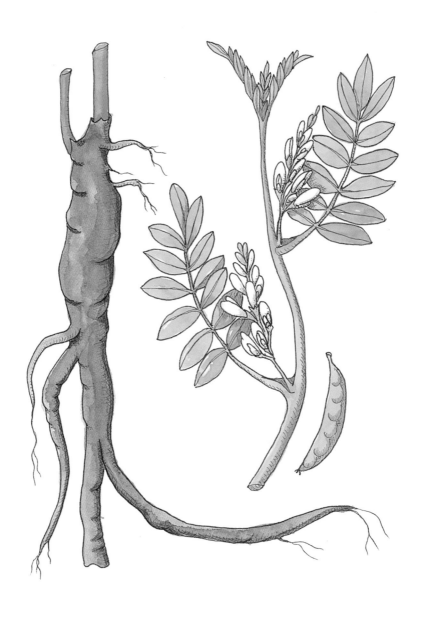

LICORICE

these that are cut and dried for processing into that precious black nec-tar, usually rendered into solid sticks or candies, we know as licorice. Licorice grows best in a warm climate as too-cool weather can interfere with the formation of its useful juice, and it prefers a sandy soil near a stream (licorice is usually not found in the wild more than 50 yards from water). At the end of a licorice plant's third season, the roots are ready to be taken up, washed, trimmed, and either sold in their entirety or cut into shorter lengths and dried. Would I honestly urge you to plant some? Not really: the processing is laborious indeed. Better to arm yourself with a packet of licorice drops come winter (it was in Holland in the sev-enteenth century that the familiar licorice pastille was born) and suck one furiously should a cold attack.

❦ 44. Lovage ❦
Levisticum officinale

"Time to carry home
the last of the flowering year . . .
here's lovage yet—but little rue . . ."

—Catherine Rogers, "Crone," 2005

L ovage, a brawny lug of a member of the *Apiaceae* family, looks like nothing so much as a stand of celery on steroids, although it is actually a cousin to anise, dill, caraway, cumin, and fennel. Native to the mountainous regions of the Mediterranean, southern Europe, and Asia Minor, and also known commonly as "Sea Parsley," "Love Herb," and the wildly evocative "Love Rod," the Greeks called it *ligustikon* and the Romans *ligusticum*, as it apparently grew rampantly in ancient Liguria. The Latin *Ligusticum* was, for some reason, transmuted to *Levisticum*, then becoming *luvesche* in Old French, the heartrending *loveache* in Middle English, and, finally, our modern "lovage." Celtic legend held that if lovage was dug up on Good Friday under cover of night, it would ward off both witches and the devil, and Felix Wurtz, the sixteenth-century Swiss physician, maintained that "if lovage roots are dug while the sun is passing over the sign of Aries, and they are fastened around the neck, they will make the approved remedy for atrophy and decline of the limbs."

However, despite the above, there is a peculiar absence of mythical herbal application in lovage's past, Mrs. Grieve giving this typically brusque assessment in her *Modern Botanical* of 1931: "It is sometimes grown in gardens for its ornamental foliage, as well as for its pleasant odour, but it is not a striking enough plant to have claimed the attention of poets and painters, and no myths or legends are connected with it." Lovage was, however, another of the useful food plants grown by Charlemagne in his imperial garden in the ninth century A.D., Hildegard

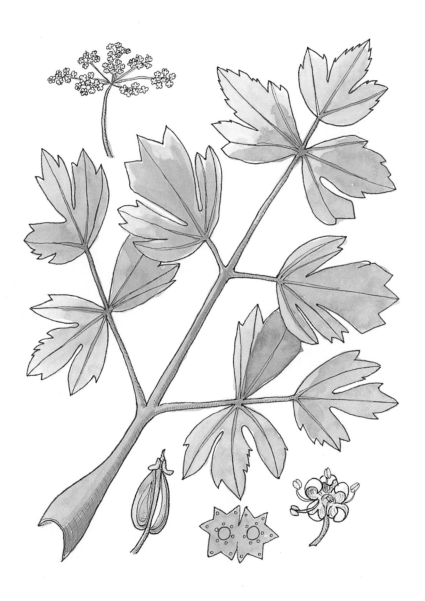

LOVAGE

of Bingen recommended it for sore throat in the eleventh century, and Mrs. Grieve opines it "... was much used as a drug plant in the fourteenth century, its medicinal reputation probably being greatly founded on its pleasing aromatic odour," also going on to say, however, "It was never an official remedy, nor were any extravagant claims made, as with Angelica, for its efficacy in numberless complaints."

Despite this humble estimation, all parts of lovage—root, stalk, leaf, and seed—were used in medieval and Renaissance Europe to treat digestive and respiratory ailments, rheumatism, bronchitis, and urinary tract infections. In 1653, Culpeper reports of lovage: "It opens, cures, and digests humours, and provokes women's courses and urine ... takes away the redness and dimness of the eyes ..." and "... removes spots and freckles from the face," with the Irish herbalist John K'Eogh concurring in 1735, in nearly plagiaristic fashion, "... [it] provokes urination and menstruation, clears the sight, and removes spots, freckles and redness from the face." In 1763, American herbalist John Sauer attributes these properties to lovage's "... warm, dry nature and ... its numerous oily, volatile, alkaline salts," with the reluctant Mrs. Grieve finally admitting in 1931, "The roots and fruit [seeds] are aromatic and stimulant, and have diuretic and carminative action."

Mrs. Grieve's lowly assessment aside, lovage *is* a striking perennial plant, hardy to USDA zone 4, and often growing to 6 feet tall, with hollow ribbed stalks similar to celery or angelica, glossy, toothed leaves, large umbels of greenish yellow flowers, and tiny oval seeds. Plant lovage in fertile soil in full sun with sufficient room to spread, cut back the flower stalks to encourage growth, and each spring should find this statuesque food plant hale and hearty. Most gourmets feel that lovage has a taste somewhere between celery and parsley, with roots, stems, leaves, and flowers all being edible. Historically, lovage stalks were candied much like angelica and consumed as a "sweet," and the young leaves are excellent in salads. However, I recommend the stalk and leaf tops as making the perfect aromatic bed and blanket for a roasted sea bass or salmon or such, imparting to it an excellent celery-esque green savor.

☿

❧ 45. Marigold ❧
Calendula officinalis
Tagetes spp.
Glebionis segetum

"Ye gold flour is good to sene
It makyth ye syth bryth and clene
Wyscely to lokyn on his flowers
Drawyth owt of ye heed wikked hirores."

—Odo Magdunenis, *De Viribus Herbarum*
(Macer's Herbal), twelfth century

Although there are at least a hundred wild species of marigold, all members of the greater *Asteraceae* or *Compositae* family, and, natively, as far flung as the Mediterranean, the Middle East, Mexico, Central America, and Asia Minor, there are three main constituents, the "Corn" marigold, *Glebionis segetum* (formerly *Chrysanthemum segetum*), the "Mexican" (or "French" or "African") marigold, *Tagetes* spp., and the "English" or "Garden" marigold, *Calendula officinalis*. Here we will stop briefly to discuss the first two, and then we will turn our rapt attention to the third. The "Mexican" marigold, mainly *T. erecta* and *T. patula*, is native to Mexico and Central America alone, and was historically employed there for a bevy of magical, religious, and medicinal applications, most notably in connection with the *Día de los Muertos* ("Day of the Dead"). Their first recorded use appears in the *de la Cruz-Badiano Aztec Herbal* of 1552, and they were carried first into Spain and Portugal, and then on to France, Africa, and, in the case of *T. patula*, famously India, by the earliest returning *conquistadores*. *Glebionis segetum* is native to the eastern Mediterranean but was widely naturalized in western and central Europe with the earliest farming to the point of such invasiveness that Alexander II, the thirteenth-century Scottish king,

MARIGOLD

decreed that for every plant a farmer allowed to seed, he would be fined one sheep.

However, it is to the "English" or "Garden" marigold, *Calendula officinalis*, the "official" marigold of pharmacopoeias, to which we will turn here. Antiquely native to Egypt, *Calendula* was brought into culture in the Greco-Roman period sometime before the fifth century B.C. Because the marigold blooms year-round in southern Europe, it was dubbed *Calendula*, from the Latin *calends* (deriving from *calare*, "to call"), referring to "the first day of the month" when the parish priest would call the local citizenry together to apprise them of the "calender" of that month's sacred events. "Marigold" is a corruption of the Anglo-Saxon *merso-meargealla*, in reference to the marigold's cousin, the marsh marigold. Popularly called "Golds" or "Ruddes" ("Reds") by the earliest British herbalists because of their exotically burnished coloring, *Calendula* was apparently notable for its propensity for closing and opening its petals with the setting and rising of the sun. Shakespeare relates in *The Winter's Tale*, "The Marigold that goes to bed wi' th' sun, / And with him rises weeping," while Rembert Dodoens states in his *A Niewe Herball* of 1578, "It hath pleasant, bright and shining yellow flowers, the which do close at the setting downe of the sunne, and do spread and open againe at the sunne rising." In the eighteenth century, Carl Linnaeus proposed an even briefer timetable: nine in the morning till three in the afternoon.

However, the most interesting belief concerning marigolds was their purported ability to literally follow the sun with their faces, with Marguerite de Valois, the prominently promiscuous wife of Henry IV of France, choosing the marigold as her armorial device in the sixteenth century, accompanied by the politically astute if sensually inaccurate motto, *"Je ne veux suivre que lui seul"* ("I wish to follow him alone,") and Charles I of England poignantly opining in his *Meditations* of the seventeenth century, "The marigold observes the sun, / More than my subjects me have done." Also commonly known as "pot" marigold, as, according to British historian Thomas Fuller in his *Antheologie* of 1655, the marigold was ". . . the Herbe Generalle in all pottage," John Gerard further advises in 1597 that ". . . no broths are well made without dried Marigold", then adds, with a clucking of his tongue, no doubt, that *Calendula* was alternately known as "Jackanapes-on-horsebacke," although only by "... the vulgar sort of women."

The sunny truth about marigolds is that, herbally, their petals are as brilliant as their hue, boasting healthy doses of triterpenoid esters (impressively anti-inflammatory), the carotenoids flavoxanthin and auroxanthin (exceptional antioxidants and the source of that gregarious coloration), as well as saponins, resins, and essential oils. Applied externally, marigold ointment is a remarkable healer of wounds, lacerations, scars, and such, and is a useful treatment for skin conditions such as acne, dermatitis, and eczema. Interiorly, being anti-inflammatory and antimicrobial, a decoction of marigold will help counteract digestive bacterial, fungal, and viral inflammatory conditions while bolstering the lymphatic and immune systems. In fact, recent studies have shown that, due to *Calendula*'s lethal effect on the viral enzyme reverse transcriptase (currently targeted by drugs like AZT), marigold flower extract can actually inhibit the replication of the HIV-I virus, and low concentrations of organic extract of *Calendula* have been shown to protect up to 90 percent of cells from destruction attributable to HIV.

William Rhind says of the sparkling marigold in his *A History of the Vegetable Kingdom* of 1865, "Though common, and hardy, and prolific as any weed, its deep orange disc is by no means devoid of beauty." Cheerfully self-seeding annuals, marigolds are available in all kinds of extroverted shades, stripings, and frillings, from the sunniest yellows to dazzling oranges and crimsons, and, for those of you who find those tones a mite too effusive, a marvelously subtle ivory/white, marketed under the names 'Sweet Cream' and 'French Vanilla.' Marigolds of any description are a cultural snap: sow (or let them self-sow) and watch them prosper, flowering from June right till frost. As noted, the dried petals make a vibrant addition to a pot of soup or stew, but allow me to leave you here with a superb recipe for an extremely efficacious ointment: melt half a cup of petroleum jelly over low heat in a double boiler, add a handful of dried *Calendula* petals, heat on low for an hour, strain, pour into a jar, and apply healingly to your next cut or abrasion.

Marjoram 'Creeping Golden'

✣ 46. Marjoram 'Creeping Golden' ✣
✣ 47. Oregano ✣
✣ 48. Oregano (Cuban) ✣
Origanum spp.
Plectranthus amboinicus 'Variegatus'

"The lily I condemned for thy hand,

And buds of marjoram had stol'n thy hair;

The roses fearfully on thorns did stand,

One blushing shame, another white despair . . ."

—William Shakespeare, Sonnet 99, 1609

While this is a clear case of herbal identity theft, I find it devilishly difficult to identify the true culprit, as both marjoram and oregano, members of the genus *Origanum* in the greater *Lamiaceae* or mint family, have apparently masqueraded as one another since man was able to sit up and take nourishment. *Origanum* derives from the Greek *oros*, "mountain," and *ganos*, "joy," and, therefore, enchantingly translates to "joy of the mountain," upon which chalky flanks these herbal siblings grow natively through various parts of the Mediterranean and Eurasia. In truth, while marjoram is an "oregano," oregano is not a "marjoram," although it has been regularly and historically regarded as such. To wit, a sampling of this mind-boggling herbal bog: botanically, culinary oregano, also known as "wild marjoram," is *O. vulgare*, and marjoram (sometimes "sweet marjoram") is *O. majorana*, although, of course, 'Creeping Golden' marjoram, the type I will recommend here, is botanically *O. vulgare*. Other constituents in this perplexing family include "pot" marjoram (*O. onites*)—also called "Italian" or "Cretan" oregano—"Greek" oregano (*O. vulgare hirtum*)—the culinary champ of the family, also called "Winter" marjoram, "Syrian" or "Egyptian" oregano (*O. maru*), and "Spanish" oregano (*O. vivens*). And just to confound matters further, an entirely different plant form,

Plectranthus amboinicus, is known as "Cuban" oregano, and in Spain, Mexico, and Jamaica, *Poliomintha bustamanta, Lippia graveolens,* and *Lippia micromera,* although totally unrelated, are all marketed as types of "oregano."

Greek legend held that the sweet, balsamlike scent of oregano was created by Aphrodite as a symbol of joy, and in parallel myth, the Romans believed Venus left her perfume lingering in marjoram as a reminder of her beauty. The ancient Greeks popularly planted "marjoram" (although, of course, it could well have been any of the "oreganos") on the graves of their dear deceased to ensure eternal peace, apparently incanting, "May many flowers grow on this newly built tomb: not the dried up Bramble, or the red flower loved by goats; but Violets and Marjoram . . . ," and both the ancient Greeks and Romans bestowed wreaths of "marjoram" on wedding couples as symbols of devotion and honor. Herbally, the Greeks made extensive use of "marjoram," both internally and externally, for wounds, poisonings, convulsions, and dropsy, and were even known to graze their cattle in fields of oregano, in the belief that it produced tastier meat.

John Parkinson, among others, identifies "marjoram" as the *Amaracus* referenced by Theophrastus, Dioscorides, and Pliny, popularly employed in the wound-healing *unguentum Amaricinum,* although, naturally, Galen demures and insists on connecting *Amaracus* to *O. maru.* The Flemish herbalist Rembert Dodoens suggested in 1554 that smelling marjoram "mundifieth the brayne . . . ," John Gerard maintained in 1597 that "orangy is very good against the wambling of the stomacke . . . , " and Parkinson reported in 1629 that "the sweete marieromes are not only much used to please the outward senses in nosegays, and in the windows of houses . . . but are also of much use in Physicke, both to comfort the outward members, or parts of the body, and the inward also . . ."

We now know it is the phenols carvacrol, thymol, and rosmarinic acid, as well as the flavonoids present in the plants we identify as "oregano" in the *Origanum* clan, that add up to a truly phenomenal display of antiviral, antiseptic, anti-inflammatory, antimicrobial, and, best of all, antioxidant power. In 2001, USDA Agricultural Research Service plant physiologist Shiow Wang and the Chinese scientist Wei Zheng put

OREGANO

OREGANO (CUBAN)

39 herbs to the antioxidant test, with oregano—specifically, oregano's impressive rosmarinic acid content—copping the crown, demonstrating 42 times more antioxidant potential than an apple, 12 times more than an orange, and 4 times more than a blueberry. Marjoram contains fewer phenols (for instance, no carvacrol) but still boasts healthy doses of both rosmarinic acid and flavonoids, as well as saponins, which promote wound and scar healing. And, although antioxidancy can vary considerably with climatic, soil, and cultural differences, infusions of both oregano and marjoram are excellent general "tonics," helping to relieve anxiety, headaches, coughs, cramps, and stomach upsets, as well as providing exceptional healing properties for external cuts and abrasions. I should also add here that ample supplies of carvacrol, which also gives these plants their signature camphorlike savor, are also found in all the non-*Origanum* "oreganos" (Mexican, Cuban, Jamaican, etc.).

Now, how to drift through all the physical variations that can identify these identity marauders? Some *Origanum* species grow to only 2 to 3 inches tall, while others sprout to a yard or more, with flower stems that may be erect or trailing, woody or nonwoody, flowers that may be purple, pink, or white, and leaves that may be round, heart shaped, elliptic, or oval, green, golden, or variegated, and hairy or smooth. The most common culinary oregano is *O. vulgare hirtum*, aka "Greek" oregano, with grayish green leaves on an erect stem growing to about a foot and, like all true culinary oreganos, possessing a white flower. My favorite marjoram is the type 'Creeping Golden' (*O. vulgare* 'Aureum'), with very golden elliptical leaves and a marvelous ground cover habit, although the general-issue marjoram (*O. majorana*) has oval, dusty green leaves, with both boasting small white flowers.

And here I am compelled to add my final complication to this morass-like scenario by introducing the stunning non-*Origanum* "oregano" *Plectranthus amboinicus*, or "Cuban oregano," into your universe, since a more beautiful or savory plant would be difficult to find. Also known under the aliases "Spanish thyme," "Indian borage," "Mexican thyme," and "Mexican mint," Cuban oregano is, as is typical in this dissembling clan, actually a native of Southeast Asia, and, especially in the 'Variegata' variety, is as vivacious as a *Coleus*, to which it is related.

Large, fleshy, green leaves are vividly marginated in white and, with a lovely semivining habit, this is a truly delightful plant to keep on a sunny kitchen windowsill in winter. Additionally, the fleshy stems root in a thrice and grow like topsy with minimal care, with a marvelous, penetrating scent somewhere between oregano and sage.

In the end, the weary "oregano" truth is, according to herb expert Dr. Arthur O. Tucker, coauthor of *The Big Book of Herbs*, "it's best to think of oregano as a flavor rather than a genus or species." As we have revealed, members of the *Origanum* family can vary broadly in taste and health benefits—some superb, some not so—while also falling victim to the whims of weather, soil, climate, etc. Conversely, there's that whole tribe of "oregano" imposters that, as they all contain carvacrol, may walk their own horticultural walk, but, culinarily and antioxidantly, insistently talk "oregano" talk. Culturally, the "true oreganos" are perennial, unfussy, and hardy to about USDA zone 5, marjorams are generally treated as annuals, and Cuban oregano is definitely a tender tropical (but do haul a potful in for the winter). At its best, oregano is a marvelous spicy herb without which Italian and Greek cuisine would be impossible, while marjoram is sweeter, with a slightly minty, citrusy savor, and Cuban oregano offers its own strong, sagelike statement. And, as described, a good many of them are mightily good for you. I say, if you have the space, plant all three types—you'll figure out how to employ them. However, let me just leave you here with a vision of a plump hen rubbed with garlic, salt, pepper, lemon, and marjoram or oregano, and then popped on the grill.

❧ 49. Marsh Mallow ❧
Althaea officinalis

"With many a curve my banks I fret
By many a field and fallow,
And many a fairy foreland set
With willow-weed and mallow."

—Alfred, Lord Tennyson, "Song of the Brook," 1887

The marsh mallow, a member of the *Althaea* genus in the greater *Malvaceae* clan, and cousin to cotton, okra, hibiscus, hollyhock, and rose of Sharon, is native to Europe, North Africa, and Asia, and is now widely naturalized in North America. Typically found growing on the banks of rivers, in salt marshes, and by the sea, as long ago as 2000 B.C. the Egyptians were mixing the marsh mallow's mucilaginous root with honey to produce what certainly must constitute one of man's first confections. The mallow was held in such high esteem by the ancient Greeks that, along with the asphodel lily, it was venerated as the most sacred sacrificial plant at the temple of Apollo Genetor on Delos, in which no blood sacrifices were permitted. *Malvaceae* derives from the Greek *malake*, "soft," from the family reputation for softening and healing, and *Althaea* originates in the Greek *althos*, "remedy," also in reference to this plant's curative powers.

Aside from medicinal applications, mallows also comprised both a notable delicacy, primarily in the form of young leaves and shoots, on antique Roman tables, as well as an invaluable food source, particularly the root and particularly in Syria, Greece, and Armenia, in times of famine, the Bible reporting in Job 30:3–4: "For want and famine they were solitary . . . Who cut up mallows by the bushes, and juniper roots for their meat." Virgil ponders the fondness of goats for mallow foliage in his *Eclogues* of the first century B.C., while in the first century A.D., Pliny the Elder maintains, "Whosoever shall take a spoonful of the Mallows shall that day be free from all diseases that may come to him."

The poets Horace and Martial both extolled the marsh mallow's laxative properties, and Culpeper devotes a long paragraph to the marsh mallow's "government and virtues," praising it, among other "virtues," for, ". . . hard tumors and inflammations . . . roughness of the skin, scurf, or dry scabs on the scalp . . . scalds and burns . . . coughs, hoarseness, shortness of breath, and wheezing . . . " as well as ". . . hurts, bruises, falls, blows, sprains, or disjointed limbs . . ." Mrs. Grieve reports in 1931 that "preparations of Marsh Mallow, on account of their soothing qualities, are still much used by country people for inflammation, outwardly and inwardly," and she judges a sweet paste made from the roots to be ". . . emollient and soothing to a sore chest, and valuable in coughs and hoarseness." Marsh mallow roots, which contain starch, mucilage, pectin, antioxidant flavonoids and phenolic acids, sucrose, and asparagine, are still employed herbally in sweetened decoctions for coughs and sore throats, and, mixed with salve, as a healing ointment.

That gummy thing so familiarly flaming at the end of your campfire stick was first invented in France around 1850, when French confectioners used marsh mallow root sap as a binding agent for egg whites, corn syrup, and water, resulting in a dual-action sweetmeat/throat-soother known as *pâte de guimauve*. By 1900, marshmallows were being mass manufactured, their makers, however, quickly eliminating the marsh mallow root from their ingredient list as being too costly, bizarrely leaving only this sweet's name to identify its herbal roots. Today, "marshmallows" are made from a decidedly unhealthy combination of corn starch, modified food starch, sugar, gum, and gelatin or whipped egg whites.

The marsh mallow is a pretty plant, impressively hardy to USDA zone 3 and growing from 3 or 4 feet high, with roundish, 3- to 5-lobed, irregularly toothed, thick, velvety leaves, and that typical appealing "mallow" 5-petaled flower, generally in a white-blushed-with-pink hue. However, to be honest, there are far comelier mallows out there to plant in your garden, and I can't really see most of you whipping up a batch of marsh mallow root salve on a Saturday. But do see if you can identify it in the wild in your neighborhood: if you do, go and investigate, recollecting this fascinating herb plant's legendary employments, and perhaps limiting your acquaintance of the manufactured type to an annual Easter chick.

Marsh Mallow

MEADOWSWEET

❊ 50. Meadowsweet ❊
Filipendula ulmaria

"The meadow-sweet flaunts high its showy wreath,
And sweet the quaking grasses hide beneath."

—John Clare, "Summer," 1835

lso known historically as "Queen of the Meadow," "Pride of the Meadow," "Meadwort," and "Bridewort," fragrant meadowsweet has decorated the meadows and moist banks of Europe and western Asia for millennia and is now thoroughly naturalized in North America. This airy plant's botanical name *Filipendula* derives from *filum*, "thread," and *pendulus*, "hanging," describing meadowsweet's root tubers, which, characteristically, hang on fibrous root filaments, while *ulmaria* connotes "elmlike," which meadowsweet clearly is not, some botanists feeling this to be an allusion to meadowsweet's somewhat elmlike crinkled leaves, while others base the reference on meadowsweet's salicylic acid content, the same pain-relieving compound found in slippery elm. "Queen" and "Pride of the Meadow" refer to meadowsweet's preference for adorning damp low-lying fields and "Bridewort" to its characteristic employment as a strewing herb at wedding ceremonies, John Gerard reporting in the sixteenth century that "the leaves and floures of Meadowsweet farre excelle all other strowing herbs for to decke up houses, to strawe in chambers, halls and banqueting-houses in the summer-time, for the smell thereof makes the heart merrie and joyful and delighteth the senses." John Parkinson related in the seventeenth century that "Queen Elizabeth of famous memory, did more desire it than any other sweet herb to strew her chambers withal."

Traces of meadowsweet were found ornamenting the cremated remains of three humans, two pigs, and possibly a dog in a cairn at Fan Foel, Carmarthenshire, in Wales, dating to 2000 B.C., and precisely the same Bronze Age burial ritual, involving cremated bone, pottery, and meadowsweet flowers in a stone cist, has been identified at both the Orkney Islands and Perthshire, Scotland. Additionally, Bronze Age vessels unearthed at Ashgrove, Fife, and North Mains, Strathallan, in Scotland, demonstrate remnants of meadowsweet pollen, probably in relation to the antique practice of flavoring meads and ales with it (thus "Meadwort"). John Gerard reports in the seventeenth century that "meadowsweet, water-mint, and vervain were three herbs held most sacred by the Druids," and in the *Four Branches of the Mabinogi*, the Welsh mythological tales dating to about 1000 A.D., the magician Gwydion famously created a spouse named Blodeuwedd ("flower face") out of oak blossom, broom, and meadowsweet for his nephew, Lleu Llaw Gyffes. Additionally, in the "Knight's Tale" from Chaucer's *Canterbury Tales* of the fourteenth century, meadowsweet, aka "Meadwort," is noted as one of fifty ingredients in a beverage called "save," and it is still a standard element in many herb-infused ales and beers.

Decoctions or infusions of meadowsweet are traditional treatments for soothing the mucous membranes of the digestive tract, reducing excess acid-ity, and easing nausea, as well as serving as a comforting therapy for colds and flu. The powerfully antioxidant flavonoids present in meadowsweet include the flavonol glycosides rutin, hyperin, and spiraeoside, as well as quercetin, kaempferol, and the phenol glycoside gaultherin. In 1897, Felix Hoffmann successfully extracted a viable synthetic version of salicin from meadowsweet, which caused less digestive upset than the plant's natural content of salicylic acid. This remarkable new drug, formally known as "acetylsalicylic acid," was ultimately dubbed "aspirin" by Hoffman's employer, the Bayer company, "aspirin" originating from meadowsweet's prior botanical name, *Spirea ulmaria* ("a" for acetyl and "spirin" from *Spirea*).

As noted, meadowsweet is a charming perennial plant with extremely sweet-scented, white-to-pink flowers clustered in graceful cymes, and fernlike leaves, dark green above and whitish and downy below, growing on erect, furrowed stems to 4 feet tall. Mightily hardy to USDA zone 3, meadowsweet will cherish a moist soil and prefer a semishady environ-ment, where it would make a wonderfully fragrant cloud of a naturalistic planting near a stream or pond. The flowers are possessed of a subtle almond flavor, and an infusion of them sweetened with honey makes a marvelous tonic, hot or cold, for either a chilly winter's eve or a sultry summer's day.

🎋 51. Mullein (Great) 🎋
Verbascum thapsus

The seeds of the great mullein, which are both narcotic and poisonous, were historically tossed into ponds and streams by Native Americans to stun fish for easier catching.

Great mullein, known by a throng of historically redolent nicknames such as "Torches," "Our Lady's Flannel," "Candlewick Plant," "Jupiter's Staff," "Beggar's Blanket," "Feltwort," and "Hag's Taper," is native to Europe and temperate Asia and is currently naturalized in eastern North America to the point of weediness. *Verbascum* is thought to be a corruption of the Latin *barba*, "beard," in allusion to the great mullein's shaggy foliage, with "mullein" deriving from the Old French *molene,* apparently in reference to a bovine and equine "scab," against which a poultice of the leaves was anciently thought to be effective. The "flannel" and "felt" references are based in great mullein's large downy leaves; the "rod" and "staff" ideas come from its impressive stature; and "torch" and "taper" stem from both a resemblance and a related mode of employment. As Rembert Dodoens reported in his *Niewe Herball* of 1578, ". . . the whole toppe, with its pleasant yellow floures sheweth like to a wax candle or taper cunningly wrought," and as Parkinson elaborated in 1629, ". . . the elder age used the stalks dipped in suet to burne, whether at funeralls or otherwise."

Great mullein was carried as a talisman by Ulysses to ward off the wiles of the enchantress Circe, and Agrippa, first-century-B.C. general to the Roman emperor Caesar Augustus, maintained its fragrance could overpower demons. Dioscorides prescribed a tisane of mullein root as a treatment for "laxes and fluxes of the belly" in his *De Materia Medica* of the first century A.D., a sentiment echoed by Culpeper in 1653, who further adds, ". . . a decoction, if drunk, is profitable for those that are bursten, and for cramps, convulsions, and old coughs." Great mullein also saw broad employment as a poultice for sores and hemorrhoids, but it was its efficacy as a treatment for pulmonary and consumptive complaints that was its chief herbal triumph, although it was extremely important to strain any decoction or infusion through muslin before imbibing to remove any "hairs," which could cause nearly intolerable irritation.

Modern medicine confirms at least this latter application, and *Verbascum* flowers were included in the *United States National Formulary* from 1916 to 1936 as one of the ingredients recommended for pectoral complaints. Chemically, with ample swats of saponins, mucilage, flavonoids, and glycosides, great mullein combines the expectorant action of its saponins with the slippery soothing action of its mucilage, making it effective indeed for treatment of hoarseness, bronchitis, asthma, and whooping cough, and with consumptives appearing to benefit greatly from an infusion of the fresh leaves boiled in a pint of milk, strained, and given warm, thrice daily. Dr. Fernie asserts in 1914, "The dried leaves . . . smoked in an ordinary tobacco pipe will completely control the hacking cough of consumption." It is also the saponins, mucilage, and tannins contained in the flowers and leaves that contribute to this plant's soothing topical qualities.

Despite its nearly invasive ubiquity in dry ditches throughout much of the world, great mullein is saved from mere weediness by the sheer majesty of its habit, its downy gray form and sunny spike rising to 6 feet or more, making it a superb addition to the rear row of even the finest mixed border. As a biennial, only foliage will appear the first year in the form of a large, silvery rosette, from which will sprout the elegant, flaming taper in the second year. If allowed to seed, great mullein will endlessly propagate itself in the same pattern and, interestingly, great mullein seeds maintain their germinative powers for up to a hundred years, and each plant is capable of producing up to 240,000 seeds. Would I actually plant some? If I had a dry border in which tall and yellow-with-silvery foliage was an attractive description, absolutely. But mainly, if I had a chest complaint, I wouldn't hesitate to go out and harvest some leaves and find myself either a pipe or a pint of milk (remember to strain!).

MULLEIN (GREAT)

❧ 52. Mustard ❧
Brassica (Synapsis) spp.

"Sympathy without relief
Is like to mustard without beef."

—Attributed to Samuel Butler, *Hudibras* (1663–1678)

There are 40 known mustard members of the *Brassica* family, but the most commonly cultivated forms are white mustard (*B. hirta* syn. *Sinapsis alba*), Indian or brown mustard (*B. juncea*), and black mustard (*B. nigra*), differentiated mainly by the color of their seeds. "Mustard" derives from the Latin *mustum ardens*, "fiery wine," in reference to the custom of mixing mustard's spicy ground seeds with *must*, newly fermented grape juice. *Synapsis*, this herbal plant's alternate botanical name, originates in the Greek *sinapi*, "that which bothers the eyes," for what I am assuming are obvious reasons. White mustard is native to the Mediterranean, the Middle East, and North Africa, brown mustard to Asia and the foothills of the Himalayas, and black mustard to Africa, India, and Europe. A plant of immense antiquity, it is the tininess of the mustard seed that is noted in Mark 4:31–32, in the passage in which Jesus attempts to explain the kingdom of God to the multitudes: "It is like a grain of mustard seed, which, when it is sown in the earth, is less than all the seeds that be in the earth: But when it is sown, it groweth up, and becometh greater than all herbs . . ."

Pythagoras commended mustard as a remedy for scorpion stings in the sixth century B.C. and, in the first century A.D., Pliny the Elder listed it in 40 separate medicinal remedies. We know the ancient Chinese appreciated mustard's purported aphrodisiacal qualities, the early Danes believed a sizzling potion of mustard, ginger, and spearmint would cure a woman's frigidity, and German lore counseled a bride to sew mustard seeds into the hem of her wedding dress to assure her dominance in the household. It is generally held that the Romans introduced mustard seed into Gallia in about the second century A.D., by the ninth century,

MUSTARD

French monasteries were growing mustard extensively in their apothecary gardens and, by the thirteenth century, balls of mustard were being hawked by peddlers as a condiment on the streets of Paris. By 1382, Phillip the Bold of Burgundy was so fond of mustard that he granted the armorial motto *moult me tarde*, "I wish for ardently," another clear source of this plant's current appellation, to the town of Dijon, France. The fourteenth-century Pope John XXII was such a fan of this sparky spice that he created the Vatican post of "Grand Moutardier du Pape" at the papal court at Avignon, and then promptly nominated his nephew to fill the position.

In 1629, Parkinson recommends mustard ". . . with some good vinegar added into it . . . to warme and quicken . . . dull spirits" and also ". . . to serve as sauce both for fish and flesh," but, by 1668, for some reason, mustard, as a condiment, seems to have gone out of favor. Parkinson reports: "Our ancient forefathers . . . were not sparing in the use thereof . . . but nowadays it is seldom used by their successors, being accounted the clownes sauce, and therefore not fit for their tables . . ." However, herbally, in 1664, John Evelyn is still touting mustard's "incomparable effect to quicken and revive the Spirits, strengthening the Memory and expelling Heaviness . . . ," and Culpeper advises it in 1699 for ". . . clarifying the blood . . . weak stomachs . . . gnawing in the bowels . . ." and ". . . pains in the sides or loins, the shoulders, or other parts of the body . . ." The gastronomic tide then turned again: by 1747, the House of Maille had been established in France; by 1804, Jeremiah Colman had perfected the "heatless" manufacture of dry mustard powder (which did not cause the seed to produce oil) in England; and, by 1856, Dijon resident Jean Naigeon had successfully substituted verjuice for the usual vinegar in the preparation of his mustard, giving birth to that distinctive *Dijonnaise* savor.

Modern herbalists still advocate mustard to promote good digestion, as, being an irritant, it stimulates the gastric mucous membrane and increases gastric juices, as an emetic especially valuable in cases of narcotic poisoning, and, externally, both as a rubefacient ("skin-reddener"), increasing blood flow toward the surface of the skin and, thereby, encouraging the expulsion of toxins, and as a plaster to relieve the pain of arthritic joints, rheumatism, muscle pain, etc. Black mustard was the antique seed of choice in Europe but, as the plants grow to different heights, making mechanical harvesting difficult, it has gone almost entirely out of favor contemporarily in deference to the other two types. Brown mustard (*B. juncea*) is the type currently employed in most Dijon and German mustards as well as the fiery English and Chinese mustards (although these may also contain some white mustard seed), while white mustard (*B. hirta*) alone is used in the manufacture of the mild, bright yellow "hot-dog-type" mustard so dear to ballparks. Therefore, here we will pause to laud the brown variety in particular, an ancient cross between *B. rapa* (the *Brassica* species that includes turnip, Chinese cabbage, pak choi, and broccoli raab) and *B. nigra*.

Mustard plants are mainly half-hardy but prolifically self-seeding annuals, clearly identifiable as *Brassicas* with their cruciferous, bright yellow blossoms, and are familiar inhabitants of pastures and meadows, coloring entire fields with their acid color on most any continent you can name. Would I honestly recommend you plant some? Again, yes and no. The manufacture of any sort of mustard (as in the condiment), save whipping some water into the superb English Colman's powder, is best left to the professionals, and, herbally, it is far easier to purchase the essential oil than to attempt to render it yourself. However, there are many fine cousins to brown mustard in the *B. juncea* species cultured, as one would grow collards or beet tops, for their spicy, leafy greens, and particularly some of the Asian varieties that triumphantly blur the line between spice and vegetable. If you have a vegetable plot, do, for instance, give the types 'Giant Red,' 'Purple Wave,' or 'Osaka Purple' a try: not only for their piquant taste, but also for the purple- or red-tinged visual splendor they will bring to your garden. Otherwise, I will close this chapter by urging you to spice up your life by grabbing a jar of your favorite mustard brand and slathering it briskly on a ballpark frank or succulent slab of ham or pot roast.

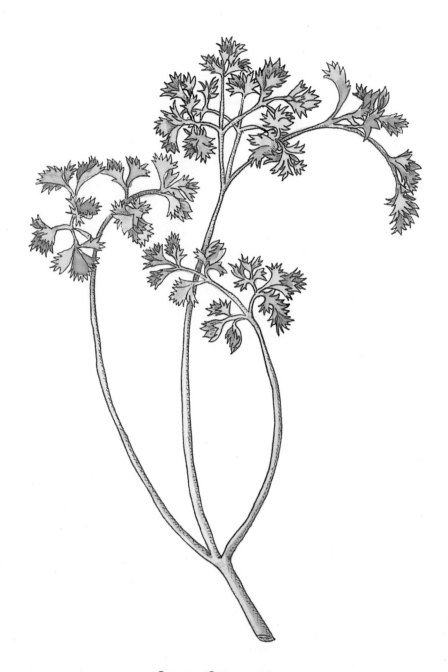

PARSLEY (CURLY-LEAVED)

❧ 53. Parsley (Curly-leaved) ❧
❧ 54. Parsley (Flat-leaved) ❧

Petroselinum crispum
Petroselinum crispum var. *neapolitanum*

"This day from parsley bed, I'm sure, was dug my elder

brother, Moore,

Had Papa dug me up before him, so many now would not

adore him . . ."

—Collected by Mary Milne-Home in
Stray Leaves from a Border Garden, 1901

Penned by the second son of the Earl of Marchmont
on the birthday of his brother, the heir

Parsley, yet another member of the *Umbelliferae* family and counting carrots, parsnips, celery, dill, and lovage among its edible cousins, is believed to be anciently native to the Mediterranean and the Middle East, with Linneaus championing Sardinia, George Bentham, the noted nineteenth-century British botanist, the eastern Mediterranean, and Augustin Pyramus de Candolle, the eminent Swiss/French botanist of the same century, Turkey, Algeria, and Lebanon. The principal varieties are our familiar curly-leaved (*Petroselinum crispum*) and flat-leaved (*P. crispum* var. *neapolitanum*) parsleys, Hamburg or broad-leaved parsley (*P. crispum* var. *tuberosum*), grown for its edible, parsnip-like root, and celery-leaved parsley (also *P. crispum* var. *neapolitanum*), grown for its edible, celery-like stalks. *Petroselinum*, parsley's botanical designation, bestowed on it by Dioscorides in the first century A.D., derives from the Greek *petros*, "rock," plus *selinon*, "celery," describing parsley's apparent historic predilection for rocky habitats. *Petroselinum* was then corrupted to *Petrocilium* in the Middle Ages, subsequently anglicized to petersylinge, and then persele and persely by the seventeenth century, and, finally, our current parsley. In 322 B.C.,

Theophrastus described the two types we will be romancing here, one with "crowded, dense leaves," the curly-leaved variety, and the other with "more open and broad leafage," the flat-leaved (Italian) type.

Greco-Roman myth held that Hera/Juno's horses supped in pastures of parsley to "make them spirited," and revelers at Greek banquets commonly adorned themselves with parsley chaplets as they thought they would absorb ill scents and alcoholic vapors. Oddly, parsley was both enjoyed and feared by the ancients, as, according to legend, the plant first sprouted from the bloody ground of the slain Greek king Archemorus, whose name translates to the rather depressing "forerunner of death," and the expression *De'eis thai selinon*, "to need only parsley," was the ancient Greek equivalent of "one foot in the grave." This morbid reputation was further enhanced by the beliefs that, according to Hippocrates, parsley was a powerful abortifacient, virgins could not plant parsley without risking impregnation by the devil, and parsley's notoriously slow germination rate was due to the seeds having to travel to hell and back at least several times before they would grow. According to Plutarch in the first century A.D., a wily but woefully underarmed Celtic monarch sent hundreds of asses saddled with parsley to greet the Greek troops advancing on his capital, causing the superstitious Greeks to flee for their lives.

On the other hand, Pliny the Elder states in his *Naturalis Historia* of 77 A.D. that "not a salad or sauce" was presented without parsley, "for the sprays find use in large quantities in broths and give a peculiar palatability to condimental foods," and, in 164 A.D., Galen praises parsley as being both "sweet and grateful to the stomach." Gerard is of the same opinion in 1597, stating that parsley is ". . . delightful to the taste and agreeable to the stomache," with Culpeper concurring in 1653, "It is very comfortable to the stomach. . . ," and adding that it is ". . . good for wind and to remove obstructions both of the liver and spleen" and "the seed is effectual to break the stone . . ." Thomas Hill, in *The Gardener's Labyrinth* of 1577, wrote with some delusion that if you desired the flat-leaved form, you tied the seeds up in a linen cloth before planting, and if you craved the curly-leafed variety, you wrapped the seeds in a ball and whacked them with a stick to crush them. William Turner, the father of English botany, clearly drinking at the same fountain as Mr. Hill, alleged in his *Gardeners' Dictionary* of 1771 that

PARSLEY (FLAT-LEAVED)

". . . if parsley is thrown into fishponds it will heal the sick fishes therein." What we now know is that parsley is nicely high in vitamins A, B, and C, potassium, iron, chlorophyll, calcium, phosphorus, niacin, and riboflavin, and, while it has carminative, tonic, and laxative qualities, it is its diuretic and detoxifying properties that are its chief values. A decoction of the root is, in fact, an admirable treatment for gravel, stone, and congestion of the kidneys, as well as rheumatism and other arthritic complaints. Parsley fruit or "seeds" also contain the volatile oil apiol, discovered by the German apothecary Heinrich Christoph Link in 1715, and first isolated and employed as a treatment for menstrual issues in 1849 by the French physicians Joret and Homolle, subsequently, and in agreement with Hippocrates, acquiring a reputation as an efficient abortifacient in small doses. However, in large doses, apiol can strongly affect the nerve centers of the head and spine, resulting in deafness, paralysis, and fatal degeneration of the liver and kidneys, so this will be another occasion for the "moderation" mantra.

Parsley also contains furamocoumarins in the coating of its seeds, which act as natural germination retardants and are, therefore, responsible for parsley's famous, usually month-long trip "to hell and back," although this period can be somewhat curtailed by soaking the seeds overnight and then planting half an inch deep, and, ultimately, thinning to 6 inches apart. A biennial, parsley will flower and set seed during its second year of growth, but, in any case, beds should be renewed every 2 years. Bizarrely, parsley is said to be fatal to small birds, injurious to other fowl, and is lethal to parrots, but is complete ambrosia to hares and rabbits, William Rhind reporting in his *A History of the Vegetable Kingdom* of 1865 that they will ". . . come from a great distance in order to indulge their taste . . . in no situation does their favorite herb escape from their depredations unless securely fenced." Flat-leaved parsley is thought to have a stronger flavor and slightly tougher consistency than the curly-leaved type, but both are indispensable in the kitchen, so my advice is plant up a pot of each to decorate both your patio and your plates: it is entirely rare that I send out a dish without a sprig or two of one or the other, for, as Thomas Hill so aptly put it in 1577, "There is nothing that doth like sweeten the mouth, as fresh and green Parcely eaten."

❧ 55. Peppermint ❧
❧ 56. Spearmint ❧
Mentha piperita
Mentha spicata

"In strewing of these herbs . . . with bounteous hands and free,
The healthful balm and mint from their full laps do fly."

—Michael Drayton, "Polyolbion," 1621

The extensive mint brood is a genus of about 25 species and 600 varieties in the greater *Lamiaceae* clan, mainly indigenous to the Mediterranean, North Africa, and western Asia, with 7 types occurring natively in Australia and 1 in North America. Greek myth famously narrates the naming of this fresh-scented family in the tale of Pluto, sovereign of the Underworld, who falls for the nymph Menthe, raising the ire of his wife, Persephone, who tries to trample her, thus inspiring Pluto to transform Menthe into a shrubby plant with a wonderfully stimulating fragrance so that he would be reminded of her comely nature each time he trod her underfoot (just like a man . . .). Peppermint, in particular, is broadly billed as the world's oldest medicine, with archeological evidence placing its initial application as far back as 8000 B.C., and dried mint leaves having been unearthed from Egyptian tombs dating to 1000 B.C. Biblically, mint appears as one of the herbal tithes of the Pharisees in Matthew 23:23: "Woe unto you, scribes and Pharisees, hypocrites! For ye pay tithe of mint and anise and cummin, and have omitted the weightier matters of the law, judgment, mercy, and faith . . ."

An ancient symbol of hospitality as noted by the great Roman elegiac poet Ovid, who, around the turn of the first century A.D., wrote of Baucis and Philemon scouring their serving board with mint before feeding the gods, mint was also popularly strewn on temple and banquet hall floors, not only to freshen the air, but also to deter vermin, who

PEPPERMINT

loathe the scent. Pliny the Elder reported further in the first century A.D.: ". . . the very smell of it alone recovers and refreshes the spirits, as the taste stirs up the appetite for meat, which is the reason that it is so general in our acid sauces, wherein we are accustomed to dip our meat." The early Romans also believed that baths scented with mint would restore both mind and body, and, in ancient Greece, where every sector of the body was characteristically perfumed with a different scent, mint was specially designated to fragrance the arms. Chaucer enjoyed ". . . a little path of mintes full and fenill greene . . ." in the fourteenth century, William Turner references "Spere Mynte" in 1568, and Gerard returns to mint's efficacy as a strewing herb in 1597, stating, ". . . the smelle rejoiceth the heart of man, for which cause they used to strew it in chambers and places of recreation, pleasure and repose, where feasts and banquets are made." John Parkinson notes ". . . divers sorts of mintes both of the garden and wilde, of the woods, mountain and standing pools or waters . . ." in 1629, further commenting in concurrence with the Romans of old: "Mintes are . . . used in Baths . . . as a help to comfort and strengthen the nerves and sinews . . ."

Culpeper recommended mint for nearly 40 ailments in 1653 for which he deemed it "singularly good," and Gerard suggested, "It is good against watering eies and all manner of breakings out on the head and sores . . ." and ". . . the stinging of wasps and bees . . ." Other medicants were convinced that the ingestion of mint would both assure the conception of male children and would act as a contraceptive when placed in the vagina, certainly giving new meaning to "minty fresh." However, mint's most notable and enduring employments were basically twofold: as an infusion, as Parkinson relates, ". . . to strengthen and comfort weak stomackes," and as an aromatherapeutic oil to relieve migraines, neuralgia, and rheumatic and muscular aches, Culpeper declaring, "Applied to the forehead and temples, it eases pains in the head . . ." Scientists have confirmed that mint's volatile oils and its impressive battery of flavonoids, phenolic acids, and triterpenes make it impressively antibacterial, antiviral, antifungal, antiseptic, carminative, and tonic. Mint tea is still a marvelous thing for stomachaches, nausea, and cramps, and minty compresses continue to be an excellent source of comfort in easing inflamed joints and sore muscles. Additionally, modern pharmacopoeias still advise a dilution of the essential oil as a wash for skin irritations and burns, and to repel mosquitoes, and the inhalation of steam infused with fresh mint leaves is recommended to relieve nasal congestion.

As noted, there are many varieties of mint. The two I recommend here are truly ancient friends: peppermint (*Mentha piperita*) and spearmint (*Mentha spicata*). Antiquely popular peppermint, a perennial hybrid of *Mentha aquatica* and *M. spicata*, is a handsome plant with square red stems, red-veined, dark green, coarsely toothed leaves, and showy, royal-purple flower wands, and I would certainly grow some just for its fine presence in a decorative border, where it will flower from July to September. Being sterile, it is propagated by root division alone; however, once you plant some, I don't think lack of it will be a problem. Spearmint is a non-red-veined version of the same with smaller leaves and flower spikes (either pink or white) and a more diminutive habit, and, certainly, its own distinctive minty savor, and has likewise been employed for its multiple herbal and culinary qualities since man first stood up and sampled a leaf.

As anyone who has grown mint knows, once established, it can become a true nuisance, sending out battalions of iron-tough invasive runners, so, therefore, it is always an excellent idea to surround your planting with a 10-inch-deep barrier of something non-biodegradable (a black plastic 5- or 10-gallon nursery pot with the bottom cut out works swimmingly). Sun or partial shade and a rich soil is all mint will need to thrive and prosper, and I can't imagine a kitchen or herb garden without a big stand of it to add a fresh jolt to a pot of fresh-picked peas or a cooling julep. However, in deference to both Pliny and my esteemed parent, I would be remiss if I did not share my father's recipe for mint sauce to accompany a roast lamb: boil half a cup of white vinegar with a quarter cup sugar until the sugar is dissolved, pour over half a cup of finely chopped mint, let stand for an hour, and ladle over a nicely pink slice.

Spearmint

PURSLANE (GOLDEN)

✤ 57. Purſlane (Golden) ✤
Portulaca oleracea sativa

"A mischievous weed that Frenchmen and pigs eat when they can get nothing else . . ."

—William Cobbett, *The American Gardener*, 1846

Those of you who are surprised by my decision to dedicate a chapter of this book to a common lawn weed are in store for further surprises that will reveal all. A member of the *Portulacaceae* family, purslane, also known as "Pigweed," "Little Hogweed," and "Pusley," is believed to be antiquely indigenous to India and the Middle East, although, somewhat mystifyingly, there now seems to be conclusive evidence dating its presence in the New World to a moment prior to 1492. Purslane seeds have been retrieved from both a Protogeometric layer in Kastanas in former Greek Macedonia dating to about 1000 B.C. and from the Temple of Hera at Samos, Greece, dating to the seventh century B.C. Hippocrates in the fourth century B.C., Dioscorides in the first century A.D., and Galen in the second century A.D. all regarded purslane as an important "cooling" herb for fever, dysentery, stomach ailments, hemorrhoids, and wounds. Pliny the Elder was so impressed by purslane's healing properties that he advised wearing the plant as an amulet would "expel all evil."

The German philosopher/saint Albertus Magnus notes purslane as a wild rather than a cultivated plant in the thirteenth century, purslane is mentioned as "procelayne" in the *Grete Herball* of 1516, and it is included by Johannes Ruellius in his *De Natura Plantarum* of 1536. It was first cultured in England in 1582, and by 1653, Culpeper is commending it as ". . . good to allay the heat of the liver, blood, reins, stomach, and hot agues . . . pains therein proceeding from heat, want of sleep, or the frenzy . . . and also for ". . . inflammations and ulcers in the secret parts . . ." John Evelyn reports in his *Aceteria* of 1699 that "purslain . . . especially the Golden, . . . quickens appetite, assuages thirst, and is very profitable for hot and bilious tempers . . . ," also remarking that it ". . . is generally entertained in all our sallets" and "familiarly eaten alone with Oyl and Vinegar."

Now for those further surprises: purslane contains a whopping 6 times more vitamin E than spinach, 7 times more beta-carotene than carrots, is nicely rich in vitamins A, B, and C, riboflavin, potassium, magnesium, phosphorus, calcium, and iron, and boasts the potent antioxidants glutathione, alpha-tocopherol, and 2 types of betalain alkaloid pigments, all offering significant benefits in the treatment of high cholesterol and triglyceride levels, heart disease, and depressed immunity. But, even more importantly, purslane contains more omega-3 fatty acids than any other leafy vegetable and is one of the very few plants that contains the long-chain omega-3 ALA (alpha-linolenic acid), with recent studies suggesting that omega-3s may have a truly important impact on depression, bipolar disorder, Alzheimer's, autism, schizophrenia, ADD, and migraines.

Jean de la Quintinye, gardener to Louis XIV, advocates purslane as "one of the prettiest plants in the kitchen garden, the red or golden being most agreeable to the eye . . ." in his *Compleat Gardener* of 1693. With thick, succulent, rounded, golden yellow leaves far larger than that crawly red-stemmed thing in your lawn, golden purslane is indeed a brilliant garden presence, and its taste is both lemony and freshly astringent, to my mind making a far more intriguing addition to a summer salad than ever-trendy arugula (and how about those health benefits?). An easy-to-grow annual with a compact, mounded habit to about 14 inches, sow in a patch and thin to 8 inches. Small yellow flowers, appearing spring through fall, open at the center of each leaf cluster for just a few hours each day, and, left to seed, golden purslane will happily self-sow for a crop next year. Pickled purslane was traditionally put up in Europe to be served as a winter *sallet*, so here I will leave you with our own Martha Washington's 1749 recipe for it: "Gather ye pursland when it . . . will snap when you break it. boyle it in a kettle of fayre water without any salt, & when it is tender, make a pickle of salt & water, . . . & when it is cold, make it pretty sharp with vinegar & cover it."

✣ 58. Rampion ✣
Campanula rapunculus

"I will allow thee to take away with thee as much rampion as thou wilt, only I make one condition, thou must give me the child which thy wife will bring into the world."

—The Brothers Grimm, "Rapunzel," 1812

Campanula rapunculus, commonly known as "Rampion," "Rampion Bellflower," "Rover Bellflower," and, yes, occasionally "Rapunzel," is broadly native to Europe, the Orient, North Africa, and northern Asia, and is surely one of the most decorative of edible plants, being cousin to the familiar campanulas of bed and border. A genus of over 300 species, the family *Campanulaceae* embraces annual, biennial, and perennial plants ranging from dwarf alpine species to sizeable woodland types growing to 6 feet or more, and *Campanula*, translating to "little bell," derives from this clan's signature bell-shaped flowers. "Rampion" originates in the Latin *rapunculus*, a diminutive form of *rapa* or "turnip," in reference to this plant's edible root, and, according to Richard Folkard, in his *Plant Lore, Legends, and Lyrics* of 1884, ". . . in the temple of Apollo at Delphi, the esculent roots of the rampion were highly esteemed as appropriate food, and were carried on golden plates." As well, fairy-tale-wise, aside from the flaxen-tressed Rapunzel's mother's famously unfortunate taste for rampion, according to Lady Rosalind Northcote in her *Book of Herbs* of 1914, there also existed an ancient Calabrian tale involving a maiden who "wandering alone in the fields, uprooted a rampion, and so discovered a staircase leading to a palace in the depths of the earth." Poetically, in 1613, Michael Drayton references ". . . rampions rare as that . . ." in "Polyolbion" ("Greatly Blessed"), his soaringly pastoral 15,000-line ode to England and Wales.

Rampion is noted by the German botanist Hieronymus Bock (Tragus) in 1552, admired by Matthias de L'Obel, botanist to England's

James I, and his assistant Petrus Pena in their *Stripium Adversaia Nova* of 1570, and, herbally, John Gerard says of rampion in 1597 that "some affirme that the decoction of the roots are good for all inflammation of the mouth and almonds of the throte . . ." However, in the main, rampion was valued as an esculent, John Evelyn recommending, "The tender roots eaten in the spring, like those of radishes, but much more nourishing," and John Parkinson reporting in 1629, "The roots are used for sallets, being boyled, and then eaten with oyle and vinegar, a little salt and pepper." However, by 1726, Benjamin Townsend, British author of *The Complete Seedsman*, states that ". . . it is to be found in only few English gardens," and, by 1931, Mrs. Grieve reveals the hard nugget of twentieth-century truth: "The Rampion formerly regularly cultivated in English kitchen gardens, and much valued, is seldom grown for use now, though its graceful flowers are sometimes seen to advantage in the borders as an ornamental plant."

Lady Rosalind concurs, writing in 1914, "Even if it is not grown for use, it might well, with its graceful spires of purple bells, be put for ornament in shrubberies." I am happy to jump on this ornamental bandwagon, rampion being, like all *Campanulas*, a lovely plant with a biennial habit, reddish purple, blue, or white flowers, and narrow crenate leaves, sprouting to 2 or 3 feet. Here, however, I am forced to include this thought from Edmund Saul Dixon's *The Kitchen Garden* of 1855, "If it once gets into your garden, you will never get it out again; and therefore it is not worth sowing the seed of so troublesome an inmate," as well as this one, in reference to the seed, from Lea and Blanchard's *The Kitchen & Fruit Gardener* of 1847: "A thimble-full, properly distributed, would sow an acre of land." As well, if grown for the culinary use of its root, rampion should not be allowed to flower, which kind of queers the decorative idea. Therefore, view this as another estimable food plant to identify in the wild, harvest for its root, and sample, peeled, boiled, and buttered, for its walnutlike savor. As Edmund Saul Dixon states, ". . . the traveler who has no radish-bed to go to, may be glad to recognize it in the course of his journey."

RAMPION

ROCKET (ARUGULA)

❧ 59. Rocket (Arugula) ❧
Eruca sativa

"If you put arugula in a salad,
it will virtually toss itself."

—Terra Brockman, "Arugula Rules!" 2000

lso known as "Rocket," "Roquette," "Rugula," and "Rucola," arugula, a cruciferous member of the *Brassicaceae* family and close cousin to watercress, the mustards, and radishes, is another of those edible plants that, like sorrel and the docks, exist in that leafy shadowland between vegetable and herb. Both "Arugula" and "Rocket" originate in this food plant's Latin botanical designation *Eruca*, which some translate to "harsh"—in reference to arugula's famously peppery bite—while others apparently identify "downy stemmed" or "caterpillar" as the references attached to this Latin root. *Sativa* is the adjective appended to any cultivated plant variety, and, in the case of arugula, wild arugula carries the designation *E. sylvatica*, referring to "forest." While it is the cultivated type that will interest us here, it is the wild variety that is believed to be the *oroth* or "herbs" mentioned in Kings 4:39: "And one went out into the field to gather *oroth*, and found a wild vine, and gathered thereof wild gourds his lap full . . ."

Arugula's tiny black (or sometimes white) seed was apparently regarded as a potent aphrodisiac by our first great civilizations, and bizarrely, in the first century A.D., Pliny the Elder advises that one ingest arugula seeds before being whipped, as he who does so will be "so hardened, that he shall easily endure the pain." John Parkinson agrees with the ancients in his *Paradisi in Sole Paradisus Terrestris* of 1629, commenting, ". . . the seede of Rocket is good . . . to stirre up bodily lust . . ." as well as ". . . provoke urine . . . ," and that it ". . . cleanseth the face of freckles, spots, and blewe markes that come by beatings, fals or otherwaies." However, much as today, arugula's principal antique employment was as a welcome pot and *sallet* herb, and it constituted an integral part of the *horta* ("greens") habitually gathered by the Greeks and Etruscans, although Galen, the great second-century-A.D. Greek "crystalizer" of Hippocratic theory, proclaimed it to be "hot and dry in the third degree" and, therefore, unfit for a solo turn in a *sallet*, instructing that it be consumed with "cold herbs" like lettuce and purslane. Arugula is romanced by St. Albertus Magnus in the thirteenth century, commented on as *roqueta* by Johannes Ruellius in his *De Natura Plantarum* of 1536, and, in 1586, the German botanist Rudolf Jakob Camerarius observes: "It is planted most abundantly in gardens . . ." In 1597, John Gerard echoes Galen, "Rocket is a good sallet herbe, if it be eaten with Lettuce, Purslane, and such cold herbes . . . ," and John Parkinson falls in line in 1629: "It is for the most part eaten with Lettice, Purslane, or such cold herbs and not alone, because of its heate and strength . . ." However, by 1726, the naysaying Benjamin Townsend reports in his *The Complete Seedsman*, "it is not now very common in English Gardens . . . ," and, by 1807, Thomas Martyn informs of arugula in his updated version of Phillip Miller's *Garden Dictionary* that "it has long been rejected."

Thereafter, it fell to Italy to be, fairly, the sole keeper of the arugula gustatory flame, until, in the late twentieth century, arugula became the gastronomic comeback kid, certainly snagging the laurels as the "celebrity green *du jour*" of the new millennium. Rich in vitamins A and C, and iron, and with a cup-sized serving clocking in at a skinny 4 calories, arugula is a simple annual to sow and grow, and its signature peppery, green, irregularly indented leaves and subtler-flavored white flowers are indispensable for spring, summer, and right-into-fall salads. Cast seed in a patch or a row, keep watered, and harvest when young, although the more mature leaves are excellent for stir-fries and such. If you have never had arugula pesto, you are in for a treat: whirl up 2 handfuls of arugula (stems removed), a handful each *parmesano* and walnuts, 1/3 cup olive oil, 2 healthy pinches of kosher salt, and some good grindings of fresh pepper in your processor. Toss with drained pasta, and swoon.

❧ 60. Rosemary ❧
Rosmarinus officinalis

"Rosemary's for remembrance, between us day and night,
Wishing I may always have you present in my sight."

—Clement Robinson, "A Nosegay for Lovers," 1584

Rosemary is another member of the greater *Lamiaceae* (mint) family, native to mainly coastal locales in southern Europe and the Mediterranean, and Lady Rosalind Northcote says of this aromatic plant in *The Book of Herbs* of 1914, "Rosemary has always been of more importance than any other herb, and more than most of them put together." "Rosemary" derives from the Latin botanical designation *Ros marinus*, meaning "dew of the sea," a reference to this shrubby herb's glistening leaves and seaside habit. In the first and second centuries A.D., Pliny the Elder, Dioscorides, and Galen all applauded rosemary's ability to "improve memory," and it was as a potent symbol of ritual "remembrance" that rosemary was widely regarded historically. Saint Thomas More, writing in the sixteenth century, reported, "As for Rosmarine . . . it is the herb sacred to remembrance, and, therefore, to friendship . . . ," and Shakespeare's Ophelia significantly opines, "There's rosemary, that's for remembrance." In 1629, John Parkinson advised the use of rosemary "at wedding, funerals, etc. to bestow among friends . . . ," with the seventeenth-century British poet Robert Herrick elaborating in verse, "Grow it for two ends, it matters not at all, / Be't for my bridal or my buriall."

In 1607, Roger Hacket, the distinguished English clergyman, sermonized in a piece entitled "A Marriage Present," "Let this rosmarinus, this flower of men ensigne of your wisdom, love and loyaltie, be carried not only in your hands, but in your hearts and heads," and rosemary was characteristically entwined into bridal coronets, Anne of Cleves, the fourth of Henry VIII's six wives, having been known to sport one to her short-lived union. Additionally, a rosemary branch, often gilded and

ROSEMARY

ribboned, was routinely presented to wedding guests as a symbol of love and loyalty, and rosemary served double duty at funerals, as mourners carried sprigs of it to gravesites both to ward off any noxious fumes that might be emanating from the corpse, and, tossing the sprigs into the grave, as a gesture of love and fidelity. In the "warding off" mode, in Spain and Italy, rosemary was vouched a general safeguard from witches and evil humors, and it was customary to burn rosemary in sick chambers and place branches in the docks of courts as a preventative for "gaol-fever." As well, it was much employed as a replacement for more costly incense in religious ceremonies, an old French term for rosemary being *incensier*.

A formula prescribed in 1235 A.D. by Elizabeth, Queen of Hungary, to "renovate vitality of paralysed limbs," and preserved to this day in the Imperial Library in Vienna, was prepared by steeping fresh, flowering rosemary tops in proof spirits, and was said to have completely cured the queen of her physical malaise. Called forever after "Hungary Water," it became the herbal rage in Europe, eventually earning itself an enduring renown in perhaps the world's favorite fairy tale, Charles Perrault's "Sleeping Beauty": "they threw water upon her face, unlaced her . . . and rubbed her temples with Hungary Water, but nothing would awaken her." It is believed that the first rosemary plants delivered into England were sent to Queen Philippa, consort/queen of Edward III, in the fourteenth century by her mother, Jeanne, Countess of Hainaut. By 1525, *Banckes' Herbal* is advising of rosemary, among many charming things, to "bynde it to the ryght arme . . . and it shall make thee lyght and mery" and to "put the leves under thy beddes heed, and thou shalbe delyvered of all evyll dremes."

In *The English Physician* of 1652, Culpeper, along with a host of other cures, commends rosemary for "inward and outward diseases . . . drowsiness or dulness of the mind and senses like a stupidness . . . benumbed joints, sinews, or members . . . a stinking breath . . ." and "to comfort the heart, and to expel the contagion of the pestilence." John Parkinson ultimately comments in 1629 that "the physicall are so many, that you might bee as well tyred in the reading as I in the writing . . ." However, in 1814, we come up against Robert Thornton's celebrated

Herbal, and this cruelly decisive rosemary truth: "This plant . . . has obtained a celebrity which it little merits . . ." and "has no claim to the high ecomiums bestowed upon this simple herb." What we know now is that rosemary mainly contains volatile camphorous oil as well as nice doses of iron, calcium, and vitamin B6 (although, oddly, dried rosemary is more nutritious than fresh rosemary). Today, the rendered oil is principally employed as a fragrant stimulant in liniments, and, aromatherapeutically, a few drops applied to the temples and such help to banish headache. However, as Culpeper cautions, "it is very quick and piercing and therefore but a little must be taken at a time." In fact, the ingestion of too-concentrated doses of rosemary oil is potentially toxic, causing spasms, pulmonary edema, coma, and even death. Therefore, my counsel is: leave the oil; cultivate the gloriously fragrant, blue-blossomed plant (full sun, light soil, hardy to zone 8) and explore a chopped handful tossed over roasting vegetables (olive oil, garlic) as a classic *fin de saison* treat.

❧ 61. Rue ❧
Ruta graveolens

"Here did she fall a tear, here in this place
I'll set a bank of rue, sour herb of grace . . ."

—William Shakespeare, *Richard II*, 1595

Hopefully we will not "rue" the moment I elected to include this pungent plant in this tome, as it arrives with a good deal of controversial baggage. Both "rue" and *Ruta* originate in the Greek *reuo*, "to set free," in reference to this herbal plant's legendary reputation as a "freer" from disease of almost any description, with *graveolens*, from the Latin *gravis*, or "heavy," (translating to "strongly scented") and *olens*, "smelling." W. T. Fernie adds in his *Herbal Simples* of 1914 that "this herb was further termed of old 'Serving Men's Joy,' because of the multiplicity of common ailments which it was warranted to cure," and rue was also known familiarly as "Herb of Grace," Canon Henry Ellacomb, in his *Plant-lore and Garden-craft of Shakespeare* of 1884, explaining, "to rue is to be sorry for anything . . . and so it was a natural thing to say that a plant which was so bitter and had always borne the name rue . . . must be connected with repentance . . . ," repentance, apparently, being just a baby step from the achievement of grace. Others, however, choose to connect this "grace"-ful designation with the fact that branches of rue (*aspergillum*) were habitually used as brushes to anoint the afflicted with holy water in the early Christian exorcism ritual known as *asperging*.

In general, the ancients viewed rue as a potent charm against witchcraft and sorcery, and it was commonly worn as an amulet in cases of epilepsy, which were thought to be instances of demonic possession. Pliny the Elder recommends rue in 84 different remedies in the first century A.D., but particularly as a strengthener of the eyes, and rue was also credited with protecting homes from plague, floors and lintels being scoured with it—in fact, heady rue acted as a fumigant to repel fleas, which were the carriers of the disease. As well, according to legend, in 63 B.C., Mithridates the Great of Pontus stubbornly survived his own attempts to commit suicide by poisoning because he had rendered himself impervious to fatal potions by the constant ingestion of rue. Everyone from Dioscorides in the first century A.D. to Nicholas Culpeper (who also recommends it for 34 other conditions, including "disorders in the head, nerves, and womb, convulsions and hysteric fits, the colic, and weakness of the stomach and bowels . . .") in 1653 seems to concur: "the seed drunke in wine" acted as a terrific counter-poison. And it is exactly here we run up against rue's large collection of "controversial baggage."

For, like other herbs of our acquaintance, in small doses, rue, due to the alkaloids and coumarins it contains, seems to be effective indeed in relaxing smooth muscles, particularly of the digestive system, relieving headaches and "hysteria," expelling poisons, and giving relief to strained eyes, in large doses, rue is an emmenagogue, abortifacient, and even an hallucinogen, and can cause both kidney and liver failure. Additionally, topically, the furocoumarins rue contains are associated with photosensitization, potentially causing blistering after contact and subsequent exposure to sunlight, John Gerard reporting, "Rue venometh the hands that touch it . . . ," and Gerard ending his rueful synopsis with, "therefore it is not to be admitted to meat, or medicine." William Rhind, in his *History of the Vegetable Kingdom* of 1865, adds a few further nails to the rue coffin with, "It has a strong, ungrateful smell, and a bitter, hot, penetrating taste."

That said, rue is a handsome, small, substantially trouble-free perennial shrub, hardy to USDA zone 4 and growing from 2 to 3 feet tall, with prettily cut, strongly fragrant blue/green foliage and small yellow or yellow-green flowers appearing from June to August. It makes a handsome foil to golden or variegated leaf varieties in the front of a shrub border or, cropped closely as one would a box hedge, a lovely low edging for a parterre bed or such. However, with this distinguished if divisive garden denizen, it's your call entirely.

RUE

SAFFRON

❧ 62. Saffron ❧
Crocus sativus

"When harvest is gone
then saffron comes on;
A little of ground
brings saffron a pound."

—Thomas Tusser, *Five Hundred Points*
of Good Husbandrie, 1580

lthough most believe *Crocus sativus*, the domesticated saffron crocus, emerged as a spontaneous mutation of the wild *Crocus cartwrightianus* sometime in the late Bronze Age (1700–1400 B.C.) on the isle of Crete, saffron-based pigments used in cave paintings in present-day Iraq have been dated to an extraordinary 50,000 years ago. Saffron was first documented on a seventh-century-B.C cuneiform tablet in the fabled library of Ashurbanipal, the last great Assyrian king, and a wall fresco at Akrotiri on the island of Santorini in Greece, dating to 1600–1500 B.C., portrays a goddess supervising the plucking of saffron crocuses. Saffron is mentioned in traditional Chinese medical texts of 1600 B.C., and, in the tenth century B.C., as a desirable sweet-smelling spice in the Hebrew Tanakh. Both the ancient Greeks and Romans prized saffron as a perfume, carrying pouches of it to render their malodorous fellow citizens less offensive and strewing it about public halls and amphitheatres, Buddhist priests elected it to color their robes at the death of Siddhartha Gautama in 483 B.C., and, in late Ptolemaic Egypt (50–30 B.C.), Cleopatra was known to luxuriate in saffron baths before her trysts in the belief they increased her desirability.

Saffron achieves legendary status in the poet Ovid's tale of the handsome Crocus, who is turned into his namesake flower by the nymph Smilax after she tires of his amorous advances, the flower's celebrated flame-colored stigmas representing the still-faint flickerings of Crocus's passion. It was probably the notably seaworthy Phoenicians who introduced saffron to the

Middle East, Iberia, southern France, and southern Italy at some time well before the birth of Christ. Oddly, saffron was popularly used to color clothing starch in seventh-century England and, by the thirteenth century, was so highly valued in Europe that pirates plying the Mediterranean would spurn shipments of gold in favor of stores of saffron. The *Crocus sativa* itself entered England in the fourteenth century during the reign of Edward III, said to have been secreted in the hollow walking stick of a returning pilgrim from the Levant, and, planted by him in Saffron Walden in Essex, it thrived to provide remedy, spice, and clothing dye to a grateful nation, the city arms of Walden ultimately bearing three saffron plants as privileged by a charter of Edward VI. The sixteenth- and seventeenth-century herbalists have a rollicking time with saffron, Gerard reporting in 1597 that it was "good for the head, and maketh the senses more quick and lively . . . ," Parkinson enthusing in 1629, "The true saffron . . . is of very great use for both inward and outward diseases . . . ," and Culpeper practically gushing in 1653, "It is said to be more cordial, and exhilarating than any of the other aromatics . . . it refreshes the spirits . . . strengthens the stomach . . . cleanses the lungs . . ." However, as Robert Thornton comments so drily in 1814, saffron is due this one wonderful caution: "It has been alleged that it raises the spirits, and in large doses occasions immoderate mirth, involuntary laughter, and other effects which follow from the abuse of spirituous liquors."

Unfortunately, *Crocus sativus* is another herbal plant that has fallen victim to modern wisdom. In the end, William Rhind, in 1865, sums it up in this manner: "As a medicine, though at one time much used and esteemed, it is now entirely disregarded." However, saffron as that exquisite spice derived from the crocus's dried stigmas is practically unequaled, as well as being barely affordable, as some 100,000 flowers are needed to produce a single kilo. The scent is heavenly: musky and fragrant of hay and honey, and, as John Evelyn advises in 1699, "Those of Spain and Italy . . . generally make use of this flower, mingling its Golden tincture with almost everything they eat . . ." In the end, saffron processing is an arduous task best left to someone else, but to encounter this pretty lavender-blossomed plant in spring, or gild a classic risotto with a pinch of its superb spice? Plant a few for the visual feast and start saving your pennies.

❧ 63. Sage (Golden) ❧
❧ 64. Sage (Pineapple) ❧
Salvia officinalis 'Icterina'
Salvia elegans

"Cur morietur homo cui Salvia crescit in horto?"

("How can a man die who grows sage in his garden?")

—Motto of the medical school of Salerno, Italy,
eighth century A.D.

Members of the extensive mint (*Lamiaceae*) family, there are over 750 varieties of sage scattered across the globe, consisting of annuals, biennials, and perennials, our familiar garden sage (*Salvia officinalis*) hailing from the Mediterranean and Asia Minor, although it has been cultivated in most of Europe since the Middle Ages. *Salvia*, sage's botanical name, was first coined by Pliny the Elder in the first century A.D. and derives from the verb *salvere*, to "save" or "heal," in reference to this herbal plant's reputation as a medical colossus. *Salvia* was corrupted to *sauge* in antique French, *sawge* in Old English, and, finally, we have "sage." There is an identifiable representation of Greek sage (*S. fruticosa*) on a fresco at Knossos on the island of Crete dating to 1400 B.C., and the use of sage's pungently scented foliage in poultices and cataplasms for the treatment of wounds, ulcers, and snakebites is recorded by Theophrastus in the second century B.C. and both Pliny and Dioscorides in the first century A.D. The ancient Romans, who considered sage to be both sacred and an excellent tonic for the brain, senses, and memory, delivered it into Britain by the fourth century A.D., and in A. D. 955, Aelfric, first Abbas of Eynsham and the most prolific of Old English writers, lists sage among the 200 trees and herbs he describes in his *Nominum Herbarum*.

As mentioned, sage was the exalted darling of early medicants, an ancient English proverb advising, "He that would live for aye, must eat

Sage in May," and an ancient French proverb avowing, "Sage helps the nerves and by its powerful might, palsy is cured and fever put to flight." *Bancke's Herbal* of 1525 says of sage, "It is marvel that any inconvenience should grieve them that use it," and John Gerard notes a number of *Salvia* species in his *Herball* of 1597, "the leaves whereof are reddish, part of these red leaves are striped with white, other mixed with white, green and red, even as nature list to plaie with such plants," and herbally commenting, "Sage is singularly good for the head and brain, it quickeneth the senses and memory, strengtheneth the sinews, restoreth health to those that have the palsy, and taketh away shakey trembling of the members." Nicholas Culpeper reports in 1653 that sage is "Good for diseases of the liver . . . stayeth the bleeding of wounds and cleaneth ulcers and sores . . . is profitable for all pains in the head . . . as also for all pains in the joints . . . cureth hoarseness and cough . . . is of excellent use to help the memory . . ." John Evelyn sums it all up nicely in his *Aceteria* of 1699: "In short, 'tis a Plant endu'd with so many wonderful Properties, as that the aciduous use of it is said to render Men *Immortal* . . ." We know now that it is sage's potent combination of volatile oils, oxygen-handling enzymes, flavonoids, and phenolic acids that give it its near-mythic antioxidant, anti-inflammatory, and antiseptic properties, and, particularly, a practically unique capacity for stabilizing oxygen-related metabolism and preventing oxygen-based damage to cells. Additionally, research published in *Pharmacological Biochemical Behavior* in 2003 confirms that sage is an outstanding memory booster, with even small doses significantly improving the immediate recall of participants in two placebo-controlled trials. Sage leaves are still officially prescribed in the *United States Pharmacopoeia*, most notably in the form of sage tea, an infusion prepared by steeping an ounce of dried sage in a pint of boiling water, its principal application being as a wash for oral infections and a gargle, sometimes mixed with cider vinegar for ulcerated throats and bleeding gums. As well, the infusion is termed a valuable mitigator of feverish delirium and the "nervous excitement" that accompanies brain and nerve disorders, an excellent stimulating tonic for stomach ailments, and a first-rate antiseptic for skin complaints and abrasions.

Of the many sage types available, here I will pause to laud one

Sage (Golden)

SAGE (PINEAPPLE)

immensely appealing "garden" variety and another variety, although not readily identifiable as a sage, that I am convinced will be of delighted interest to you. While I am tempted to offer up the dusky garden variety 'Purpurea,' with its intensely purple foliage, here, instead, I ask you to turn your attentions to a sunnier idea, the beauteous golden sage, *Salvia officinalis* 'Icterina.' Characterized by brilliant green-marginated-in-gold leaves and whorls of pretty purplish flowers, 'Icterina' is a luminous garden presence worthy of a place in any bed or border. Being a Mediterranean *habitué*, 'Icterina' will appreciate full sun and a well-drained soil and will be reliably hardy only to USDA zone 8, although some winter mulching will increase your chances of perennial success. In any case, sage plants are best renewed every 4 years or so and, while they can be propogated by seed, new plantations are easily produced by rooting shoots in autumn after flowering and then planting out in spring.

The second sage type I commend to you here is the exuberant pineapple sage (*Salvia elegans*), a subtropical variety native to Mexico and, therefore, also only hardy to USDA zone 8. Growing as a shrub to 4 or 5 feet, pineapple sage boasts bright green, defiantly un-sagelike saw-toothed leaves possessed of an amazingly strong, fruity, "pineapple" aroma, and vivid scarlet, tubular blossoms arranged in whorls on foot-long spikes, making a perfectly stunning presence in the garden. If it is hardy for you, cut stems back to about 8 to 12 inches in fall and mulch well; otherwise, as with the golden type, root cuttings over the winter (pineapple sage cannot be propagated from seed) and plant out in spring. For the pineapple sage, young leaves are lovely in summer salads, add a wonderful pineapple savor to marinades, and a handful of the crushed leaves swirled in ice water makes an ideal summer refresher. For the brilliant 'Icterina,' John Russell's *Book of Nurture* of 1460 describes sage "frytures" as being popular at medieval banquets, so why shouldn't they be at yours? Beat a cup of flour with half a cup of beer, an egg, and a pinch of salt into a batter, dip in fresh, dry sage leaves, deep-fry until puffy and browned, drain on paper towels, and serve with a honeyed vinegar dipping sauce.

❦ 65. Shiso (Purple) ❦
Perilla frutescens nankinensis 'Purpurea'

"'On the contrary,' I said, 'I have the very highest regard for matinee girls, and for you Perilla, in particular.'"

—John Corbin, "Perilla at the Matinee," 1902

Very well: the above quote has absolutely nothing to do with the food plant we are about to discuss, as, apparently, "Perilla" was also a somewhat arcane historic option in feminine appellation (see Robert Herrick's "To Perilla," circa 1640). The "Perilla" we choose to enthuse about here is yet another member of the *Lamiaceae* (mint) family, the most common species being *Perilla frutescens*, commonly known as *shiso*, native to the Orient and mainly grown in India and East Asia. Known for both its herbal and culinary applications, particularly in Traditional Chinese Medicine, perilla, known as *su*, *zi su*, or *zi su ye*, is recorded in Chinese medical texts as early as 462 A.D., *su* meaning "comforting," *zi* translating to "purple," and *ye* to "leaf." Also know commonly as "beefsteak" plant for its large purple-tinged slab of a leaf, and, in North America, as "purple mint," "Chinese basil," and "wild coleus," although it is none of these, perilla is unquestionably a recent introduction to our gastronomic and herbal lexicon. That, in combination with its, shall we say, "unique" savor, may make it unfamiliar to most of you; however, perilla's moment may have come: Harold Dieterle III, first-season winner of the cable-television reality show *Top Chef*, recently named his well-reviewed new Manhattan restaurant after this herbal ingénue, its logo being a spritely sprig of the purple variety.

Viewed as a "pungent, aromatic, warming herb," perilla's leaves, stems, and seeds are all employed in Oriental medicine for their antibacterial, antiseptic, antispasmodic, aromatic, carminative, emollient, expectorant, and tonic properties in the treatment of such diverse complaints as asthma, colds and chills, bronchitis, nausea, abdominal pain, food poisoning and allergic reactions (especially related to seafood), constipation, and "to

Shiso (Purple)

move stagnated *qi* ("personal energy")" and "redirect rebellion *qi* downward." Modern research has proven that perilla is, in fact, impressively rich in calcium and iron and has been shown to stimulate interferon activity and, thus, the body's immune system. Distilled perilla oil is an excellent source of the important omega-3 fatty acid ALA (alpha-linolenic acid), and additionally, perilla oil has been historically employed as a "drying" oil, similar to tung or linseed oil, in the manufacture of fine oil paints, helping them to fuse and blend more thoroughly and imparting to them an enamel-like smoothness.

There are both green-leaved and purple-leaved varieties of perilla, the green type called *aojiso* or *aoba*, meaning "green shiso" and "green leaf" respectively, and the purple variety called *akajiso*, meaning "red shiso," and it is to the lovely latter variety I will direct you here. A generously self-seeding annual (perennial to USDA zone 8), purple shiso is an arresting plant indeed with its large, broad, jaggedy-edged, bronzy purple leaves and pink/purple flower wands, looking approximately like the "opal" variety (*Ocimum basilicum* 'Purpurascens') of its cousin basil. Purple perilla, although a fairly unfussy sort, will positively thrive in full sun in a light-to-medium soil with a pH between 5.5 and 6. We plant it in our pastel-hued mixed borders, where it is a striking foil to white and blue blossom, and we habitually find legions of seedling volunteers the next season (let me just mention here for those of you who keep cattle or horses that ingestion of the perilla ketone contained in purple perilla can cause pulmonary edema in those animals, leading to a condition called "perilla mint toxicosis," so please be forewarned). Used to add color and punch to pickled plum and ginger among many other dishes in the Orient, purple perilla's flavor is, frankly, contentious, some people detecting notes of cinnamon or coriander or citrus or mint, while others perceive a more rank savor. My counsel would be to plant a stand in your herb or decorative garden for the ongoing glory of the plant and see how you feel about the taste.

ॐ

❦ 66. Soapwort ❦
Saponaria officinalis

"In July, Bouncing Bet came again, appearing silently, with imperceptible gradations of progress, as was her wont."

—Mary E. Wilkins, "Bouncing Bet," 1901

Related to the decorative garden "Pink" in the greater *Caryophyllaceae* family, soapwort is originally native to northern Europe and currently naturalized throughout much of eastern North America. The genus name *Saponaria* derives from the Latin *sapo*, meaning "soap," and soapwort has gone by many monikers in its long history of employment, including "Soaproot," "Latherwort," "My Lady's Washbowl," "Fuller's Herb," and, most commonly, "Bouncing Bet." "My Lady's Washbowl," "Soaproot," and "Latherwort" all originate, as does "Soapwort," in this herbal plant's most famous antique application, Nicholas Culpeper explaining in his *Herbal* of 1652, "Bruised and agitated with water, it raises a lather like soap, which easily washes greasy spots out of cloaths..." "Bouncing Bet" finds its origins in an antique name for a washerwoman, and "Fuller's Herb" in soapwort's employment in "fulling" wool (increasing its weight through a process of shrinking and beating).

Traces of soapwort have been identified on both the celebrated Shroud of Turin, purported to bear the image of the crucified Savior, and the eleventh-century-A.D. Bayeux Tapestry, depicting William the Conqueror's Norman conquests of England. Additionally, in her *Book of Herbs* of 1968, Dawn McLeod relates the tale of Lady Meade-Fetherstonhaugh, twentieth-century chatelaine of historic Uppark in England, who inherited 30 immense 1740 Italian brocade drapes, which hung there "... like distressing wreaths of damp ... pink seaweed ..." Introduced to soapwort and soon setting up a steaming cauldron-full, McLeod informs us that "not only were the ancient fabrics cleaned gently and efficiently ... the herb actually put new life into the fibres from which they were woven ..." and that "the color of the dye ... was ... restored to its original brilliance and depth."

SOAPWORT

Soapwort's legendary lather, obtained from the crushed foliage and root, is due to the saponins it contains: natural detergents that mix with both water and oil, hence their cleansing ability. Saponin-rich soapwort, in a similar "cleansing" mode, was historically recommended for a battery of antiseptic, anti-inflammatory, detergent, purgative, diuretic, expectorant, and laxative purposes, Robert Thornton reporting in his *Herbal* of 1814 that Ludovicus Septalius, the seventeenth-century Italian physician, recommended a decoction for venereal disease, and Herman Boerhaave, the great eighteenth-century Dutch botanist, extolled soapwort for jaundice and liver complaints. The 1633 edition of John Gerard's *Herball* likewise notes that soapwort was used in the treatment of syphilis, and also attests, "Some have commended it to be very good . . . applied to greene wounds, to hinder inflammation, and speedily to heale them." Additionally, soapwort was a traditional treatment for skin disorders, gout, and rheumatism. Today soapwort is still uniquely valued by antique textile restorers and is also commonly found in cough remedies, diuretics, toothpastes, gargles, and shampoos. However, long-term ingestion of saponins can cause gastric irritation, nausea, and diarrhea, so do be judicious in any internal application.

Soapwort is a perfectly charming if slightly invasive plant, and is probably naturalized somewhere near you in a roadside ditch or such, with habits ranging from low sprawling alpines like the "Rock" soapwort (*Saponaria ocymoides*) with pink-to-white flowers and hardiness to USDA zones 2 to 7, and the dwarf form 'Nana,' also with pink blooms, growing to 15 inches and hardy to zone 4, to 'Rubra Plena,' with red blossoms, growing to 24 inches and hardy to zone 3, and 'Alba Plena,' with double white flowers and growing to more than 2 feet. All boast handsome lanceolate green foliage and sweet-scented, 5-petalled blossoms. Once established, most will spread handily via rhizomes, forming lush stands of leaf and flower, and are superb choices for any sunny spot in your garden, although, oddly, soapwort is poisonous to fish, so do not plant near a pond or stream. That said, I would allow the comely blossoms of this darling of museum conservators to, as John Parkinson recounts in 1629, "deck both the garden and the house," and, after an evening of hearty banqueting, allow the macerated roots to help refresh those fine family linens.

❧ 67. Savory (Summer) ❧
❧ 68. Savory (Winter) ❧
Satureja hortensis
Satureja montana

"Keep it dry by you all the year, if you love yourself and your ease,
and it is a hundred pounds to a penny if you do not."

—Nicholas Culpeper, *Culpeper's Complete Herbal*, 1652

The genus *Satureja*, another subset of the multiherbed mint (*Lamiaceae*) family, contains over 30 species, all basically native to the Mediterranean, with *S. hortensis*, the annual summer or "garden" savory, and *S. montana*, the perennial winter savory, being the two types most generally grown for culinary and medicinal application. *Satureja*, bestowed upon this botanical family by Pliny the Elder in the first century A.D., derives from *Satureia*, connoting "for the Satyrs," as these fine-scented plants were thought to belong to them, and, according to Richard Folkard in his *Plant Lore, Legends, and Lyrics* of 1892, "matrons were especially warned to have nothing to do with [them], as the plant was supposed to have disastrous effects on those about to become mothers." Perhaps because of this priapic association, the savories had an intriguing reputation for being able to regulate sex drive, winter savory being said to decrease it when ingested, while summer savory was thought to enhance it, so one imagines that is why the summer type was preferred in most gardens. Additionally, in the first century B.C, the Roman epic poet Virgil celebrated both savories as being among the most fragrant of herbal plants and, therefore, commendable for growing near beehives.

Savory is lauded by Palladius in his *Opus agriculturae* of the fourth century A.D. and in the thirteenth century by St. Albertus Magnus, and it also rates a literary mention in William Shakespeare's *The Winter's Tale*, contestably of 1594, in the passage in which Perdita, banished to Bohemia by her father Leontes, king of Sicilia, presents blossoms to her royal

SAVORY (SUMMER)

SAVORY (WINTER)

visitors-in-disguise: "Here's flowers for you, hot lavender, mints, savory, marjoram . . ." On the North American continent, the early American botanist John Josselyn lists both summer and winter savory in his *New England Rarities* of 1672 as two of the plants introduced there by the earliest English colonists to remind them of the gardens they had left behind. Although both savories on any continent were mainly employed as culinary herbs, like most antique food plants, they did see their share of medicinal duty, in 1629 John Parkinson recommending savory as ". . . effectual to expel winde . . . ," and the reliably vociferous Nicholas Culpeper reporting in his *Herbal* of 1652, ". . . the Summer kind is . . . both hotter and drier than the Winter kind . . . It expels tough phlegm from the chest and lungs, quickens the dull spirits in the lethargy, if the juice be snuffed up the nose; dropped into the eyes it clears them of thin cold humours proceeding from the brain . . . the juice . . . dropped in the ears removes noise and singing and deafness . . ." and ". . . outwardly applied . . . eases sciatica and palsied members."

Dr. O. Phelps Brown proposes in his *The Complete Herbalist* of 1872 that "the whole herb, and especially the flowering shoots, is mildly antiseptic, aromatic, carminative, digestive, mildly expectorant and stomachic. Taken internally, it is said to be a sovereign remedy for colic and a cure for flatulence . . ." In addition, both ancient and modern herbalists are in agreement that a sprig of either of the savories applied to the sting of a wasp or a bee will provide instant relief. In the end, the savories are not powerhouses of anything in particular, with dried summer savory containing approximately 1 percent volatile oil and winter savory about 1.6 percent, both composed primarily of the phenolic monoterpene thymol, oxygen-rich carvacrol, and a smattering of triterpenic acids, including ursolic and oleanolic acid. These amount to some clear antioxidant activity, although not of an especially impressive stature, all of this adding up to mild aromatic, astringent, antiseptic, and carminative properties, and savory infusions are deemed beneficial for the occasional bout of colic, diarrhea, indigestion, or flatulence, and mild sore throats.

Summer savory (*S. hortensis*) is an annual herb, growing to about 2 feet high with oblong medium-green leaves and pretty if diminutive pink-to-blue-white flowers. It is easily raised from seed sown in spring in light soil in a sunny situation (think Mediterranean), and then thinned to about 9 inches apart. Winter savory, on the other hand, is a dwarf perennial shrub, growing to about the same height, with leaves and blossoms both sharing basically the same characteristics as summer savory, and may be propagated from seeds sown in spring in the same manner as summer savory or from cuttings and root divisions. Also displaying a preference for a sunny spot, oddly, winter savory is thought to thrive better in a poor soil than a rich one, and, in a situation that suits it, winter savory will continue happily and perennially for several years, and will then gracefully degenerate, when it will be time to root some cuttings for the following season. For their daintily blossomed habit and fragrant personality, either savory would be a welcome addition to any herb garden.

The flavor of the savories, as you might expect from the dose of thymol in their composition, is most often described as "thymy." Summer savory is thought to be "sweeter" than winter savory, and it is summer savory that is employed nearly exclusively in culinary commerce, interestingly playing a significant role in Bulgarian cuisine: instead of salt and pepper, a Bulgarian table will habitually display three condiments: salt, paprika, and savory, sometimes mixed together into *sharena sol* ("colorful salt"). John Parkinson recounts that winter savory, dried, powdered, and mixed with bread crumbs, was used "to breade their meate, be it fish or flesh, to give it a quicker relish," and Charles Cotton, in his sequel to the *Compleat Angler* of 1676, recommends dressing a trout with "a handful of sliced horseradish-root . . ." and "a handsome little faggot of rosemary, thyme and winter savoury," which is a splendid idea. So is this one: cook green beans in salted water fragranced with a palmful of savory (don't overcook!), drain, toss with a knob of butter, and top with shreds of crispy bacon if you dare.

ॐ

❧ 69. Stevia ❧
Stevia rebaudiana Bertoni

United States Congressman Jon Kyl of Arizona baldly called the U.S. FDA's 1991 ban on the use of stevia as a sweeting agent "a restraint of trade to benefit the artificial-sweetener industry."

This is an herb that makes me boil. Stevia, a member of the *Asteraceae* clan, is originally native to northern Paraguay and southern Brazil, and, known as *kaa he-e* ("honey leaf"), has been employed by the Guaraní and Mato Grosso Indians since some hazy hour in our prehistory. Adopted by the marauding Spanish *conquistadores* as *yerba dulce* ("sweet herb") and, later, by the nineteenth-century *gauchos* of the South American pampas, it was first declared a "new species" in 1899 by Dr. Moisés Santiago Bertoni, director of the College of Agriculture in Asunción, Paraguay, who named this newly discovered *Stevia* sort *rebaudiana* in honor of the Paraguayan chemist Rebaudi, who first extracted its sweet constituent. Bertoni's complete study of 1905 eulogized that "the sweetening power of *kaa he-e* is so superior to sugar that there is no need to wait for the results of analyses and cultures to affirm its economic advantage . . . the simplest test proves it."

In 1913, however, a prescient report from Germany's state laboratory noted "specimens received are of the well-known plant which alarmed sugar producers some years ago," and *here* is where this truly tawdry tale of corporate manipulation begins. By 1921, American trade commissioner George S. Brady was touting stevia as a "new sugar plant with great commercial possibilities," labeling it "an ideal and safe sugar for diabetics," and, in a memo to the U.S. FDA, stating he was "desirous of seeing it placed before any American companies liable to be interested, as it is very probable that it will be of great commercial importance." Oddly, absolutely nothing happened. In 1931, when the French chemists Briedel and Lavieille isolated stevioside, the crystalline extract that gives stevia its sweetness, United States government researcher Dr. Hewitt G.

Fletcher described it as "the sweetest natural product yet found." However, again, *oddly*, nothing happened. Around 1970, Japan approved stevia as a sweetener and flavor enhancer, and, in the last 35 years of Japanese employment, not a single case of toxic or deleterious effect has been brought to light. Yet, really oddly, in the 1980s, shortly after the Monsanto company, champion of genetic alteration, among other dubious notorieties, introduced their artificial sweetener aspartame, representatives from an "anonymous firm" lodged a complaint with the U.S. FDA against the importation and use of stevia, and, in 1991, the herb was placed on "import alert" to the extent that even *owning a plant* became illegal.

In 1994, the U.S. FDA, due to the Dietary Supplement Health and Education Act, was finally forced to modify its alert, and, currently, stevia may be sold as a "dietary supplement" but *not* as a sugar substitute, and it is *still illegal* to even hint at the "sweetening" idea in stevia imagery or advertising. Oh—and, most oddly, in 1997, Linda and Bill Bonvie, coauthors of *The Stevia Story*, revealed that although an astounding 75 percent of non-drug-related consumer complaints are directed squarely against Monsanto's aspartame, the U.S. FDA has never taken a single step in their direction. In 1997, Robert S. McCaleb, founder of the Herb Research Foundation, summed it up: "The FDA took action against stevia, not based on any proclamation by the FDA toxicologist or consumer complaints, but because of a complaint from a company that didn't want stevia on the market."

A stevia leaf is 10 times sweeter than sugar and contains about 1/10 calorie, with a teaspoon of the crushed leaves equaling a cup of the other stuff. Additionally, stevia, an easy, boisterous annual looking a bit like a tall stand of oregano with its tiny, tufty, white blossoms, has shown immense promise in treating both obesity and high blood pressure and, as stevia has a negligible effect on blood glucose levels, it is just the ticket for diabetics. Are you boiling yet? If so, find some. Grow some. Taste a stevia leaf and how startlingly sweet nature can be. Experiment. Extoll. Bring down big business.

STEVIA

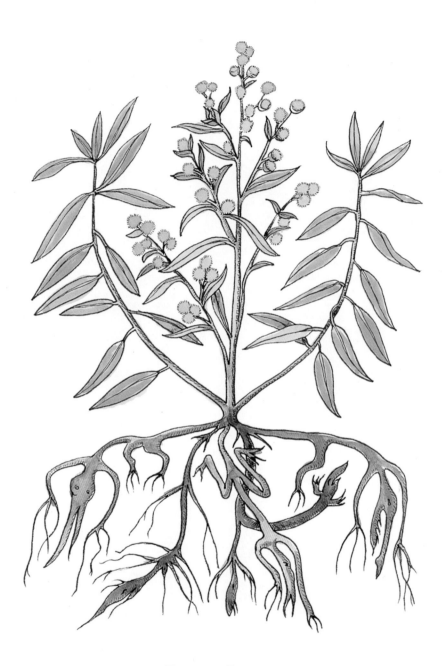

TARRAGON (FRENCH)

❧ 70. Tarragon (French) ❧
Artemisia dracunculus

"Ruellius and such others have reported many strange tales hereof
... saying that the seed of flax put into a Raddish root or sea Onion,
and so set, doth bring forth this herbe Tarragon."

—John Gerard, *The History of Plants*, 1636

Despite the seventeenth-century French botanist Johannes Ruellius's rather misguided take on its provenance, most horticulturists agree that French tarragon, a member of the *Artemisia* clan and cousin to wormwood and mugwort, far from being the wayward spawn of flax and radish, is a subtly savored herbal plant native to Mongolia and Siberia. Tarragon's species name *dracunculus*, Latin for "little dragon," finds its origin in the roots of this edible plant and their serpentine "dragon"-like habit. "Tarragon" derives from the Arabic *tarkhum*, also meaning "little dragon," by way of the French *esdragon*. Most feel tarragon's generic name, *Artemisia*, pays homage to Artemis (aka "Diana the Huntress"), Greek goddess of the moon, and the soft silvery coloration of many of this family's progeny, looking for all the world as if bathed in moonlight. Also known as "Little Dragon Mugwort" and, in French, *Herbe au Dragon*, French tarragon should not be confused with Russian tarragon (*Artemisia dracunculoides*), its far-heartier-of-habit but infinitely less tasty surrogate.

Tarragon is thought to have been introduced into Italy from the shores of the Black Sea somewhere around the tenth century A.D. Dr. E. Lewis Sturtevant states of tarragon in Europe in his *Notes on Edible Plants* of 1919 that "the first mention on record is by Simon Seth in the middle of the twelfth century," and it is believed that tarragon was carried into England in about 1548, during the sadly short reign of the boy-king Edward VII, younger half-brother of Elizabeth I. Interestingly, while most herbs have a long history of medicinal employment, tarragon is oddly lacking in much more than culinary application, John Gerard reporting in *The History of Plants* of 1636, "Tarragon is not to be eaten alone in sallades, but joyned with other herbs, as Lettuce, Purslain, and such like, that it may also temper the coldnesse of them . . . neither do we know what other use this herbe hath." Some ethnobotanists feel this phenomenon may be because tarragon loses its aromatic volatile oils almost entirely when dried and is, therefore, fairly impossible to "keep."

However, according to the *Doctrine of Signatures*, a broadly respected philosophy in medieval Europe, which held that plants reminiscent of human or animal parts—or even inanimate objects—had useful relevance to those things, it was believed that tarragon's dragonlike root signified notable effectiveness against the bites and stings of venomous creatures. Additionally, in his *Acetaria of 1699*, John Evelyn endorses tarragon as ". . . highly cordial and friend to the head, heart and liver," while in 1653 Nicholas Culpeper chimes in on an uncharacteristically lukewarm note, "The leaves, which are chiefly used, are heating and drying, and good for those who have the flux, or any preternatural discharge. It is a mild martial plant." As well, it was known that the ancient Greeks used tarragon as a treatment for toothache, modern medicine affirming that tarragon gets its pain-killing properties from the natural anesthetic eugenol.

French tarragon is not the most trouble-free herb I have ever cultured but is entirely worth the effort, as there really is no substitute for its subtle, sweet, licorice-like savor: a thing so beloved by the French that they have deemed it the "King of Herbs." Growing to about 2 feet tall with long, narrow, undivided leaves (unusual in this genus), and blossoming in August with tiny yellowish green flowers, tarragon craves warmth and sunshine and will succeed best in a hot, dry situation with adequate drainage. As well, tarragon is not known to seed and must be propagated by either root or stem division. Because tarragon loses its flavor rapidly when dried, historically, pickling was a popular way to "keep" it, and surely every kitchen deserves a big bottle of homemade tarragon vinegar to dollop here and there: stuff a half dozen sprigs into a tall bottle, fill with white or cider vinegar, cork, and steep on a sunny windowsill for several weeks.

✿ 71. Thyme (Garden) ✿
✿ 72. Thyme (Lemon 'Silver Queen') ✿

Thymus vulgaris

Thymus citriodorus 'Silver Queen'

"Thestilis for mowers tyr'd with parching heate,
Garlicke, wilde Time, strong smelling herbes doth beate."

—Virgil, *Eclogues*, 44–38 B.C.

Thyme is a genus of about 350 aromatic plants in the sprawling *Lamiaceae* (mint) family. Native to Europe, North Africa, and Asia, its earliest recorded use occurs in Sumeria in 3000 B.C., where it is noted, as in many subsequent cultures, including our own, as a powerful antiseptic. The Egyptians utilized thyme in their mummification processes and, in close parallel employment, the ancient Greeks placed it in the coffins of the dead, assuring their passage into the afterlife, and made use of it for purifying sacrifices to make them acceptable to the gods, as well as a fumigant against illness and disease and as a chief ingredient in ritual altar fires. It was also wishfully believed that the souls of the dear departed took up residence in the flowers of thyme after death. "Thyme" is thought to originate in the Greek *thumus*, either signifying "smoke" (by way of the Latin *fumos*), in reference to this herb's antique role as fumigant and sacrificial incense, or "courage," as thyme was thought to engender it with its "cordial qualities" (W. T. Fernie, *Herbal Simples*, 1914).

Of more rarified interest is Richard Folkard's pronouncement in his *Plant Lore, Legends, & Lyrics* of 1892 that the honorific "to smell of thyme" was antiquely awarded to Greek writers who mastered the "Attic" style of expression, which reigned in Greece until the fourth century B.C., introduced the definite article, infinitive, and participial clause into the language, and finally permitted the construction of complex yet elegantly bell-clear sentences. According to Folkard, this designation for "honeyed" prose derives from the fact that thyme ". . . covered Mount Hymettus, and gave to the honey made there the aromatic flavor of which the ancients were so fond . . ." Tradition also holds that thyme was a component of what has come to be known as "Our Lady's Bedstraw," which lined the Savior's cradle on that long-ago Christmas Eve. The ancient Romans, much like the Greeks and Egyptians, used thyme to purify their rooms, and soldiers were known to bathe in thyme-scented water before going into battle to engender courage, ultimately spreading it throughout Europe with their conquests. By the Middle Ages, Lancastrian ladies in England were habitually bestowing tokens of thyme on their errant knights to render them courageous and embroidering the figure of a bee hovering over a sprig of thyme onto scarves to adorn them as a symbol of, according to Folkard, the union of "the amiable and the active." And, of course, in Shakespeare's *A Midsummer Night's Dream*, Oberon gives this famous description of the forest bower of the fairy queen Titania: "I know a bank whereon the wild thyme blows, / Where oxlips and the nodding violet grows . . ."

As with many pungent herbs, particularly among the members of the mint family, thyme has had a long history of herbal application. In 1597, John Gerard recommends it for the apparently always anciently problematic "bitings of any venomous beast . . . ," while in 1629 John Parkinson claims it useful for ". . . melancholic and spleneticke diseases, as also to flatulent humors . . ." The consistently exhaustive Culpeper states in 1653 that thyme is "a strengthener of the lungs . . . an excellent remedy for shortness of breath . . . kills worms in the belly . . . provokes the terms . . . an ointment takes away hot swelling and warts . . . helps the sciatica and dullness of sight . . . excellent for those that are troubled by gout . . . to anoint the testicles that are swelled . . ." and ". . . comforts the stomach much and expels wind . . ."

We now know the volatile oil thymol is the key constituent here, and, certainly, one with which to be reckoned, as recent studies have confirmed that it is fiercely antioxidant and is capable of not only increasing the amount of DHA (docosahexaenoic acid), a notably potent omega-3 fatty acid, in brain, kidney, and heart cell membranes, but is also impressively antimicrobial against a battery of bacteria and fungi, including *Staphalococcus aureus* and *Bacillus subtilis*. Thyme also contains a healthy number of flavonoids, which only add to its antioxidant swat, and is an

Thyme (Garden)

THYME (LEMON 'SILVER QUEEN')

excellent source of iron, manganese, calcium, and dietary fiber. Today, despite its having been dropped from the *United States Pharmacopoeia*, a thyme infusion is still herbally recommended for cough and bronchitis, as well as respiratory infections in the form of a tincture, tisane, salve, syrup, or by steam inhalation.

As noted, there are many comely varieties of thyme: some carpetlike (wooly thyme, *Thymus pseudolanuginosus*), some scented of caraway (*T. herba-barona*) or orange (*T. vulgaris* var. *odoratissimus*) or lime (*T. citriodorus*), and others with golden leaves (*T. vulgaris* 'Aureus') or colorful marginations (*T. argenteus*). I will enthuse over two stellar varieties here, but I always plant five or six types in my gardens, for I am in perfect agreement with Sir Francis Bacon, who, as Dr. Fernie relates, ". . . recommends to set whole alleys of Thyme for the pleasure of the perfume when treading on the plant." The couple we will pause to laud here are that culinary champion, the common garden thyme (*T. vulgaris*), and the lovely variegated lemon thyme 'Silver Queen' (*T. citriodorus* 'Silver Queen'). Garden thyme is a truly stalwart herbaceous perennial with tiny, curled, elliptical, greenish gray leaves and wiry stems, usually growing from about 4 to 12 inches high, the leaves rich with that signature thyme fragrance redolent of pine and camphor, and pretty, diminutive purple blossoms in summer that will literally blanket the ground with vibrant color.

'Silver Queen,' growing to a similar height with an erect branching habit, is a lemon thyme cultivar that features heavenly lemon-savored and scented, deep green leaves edged in silver, and whorls of tiny, pale lilac blossoms. Either type will be perennially hardy to USDA zone 5, and both, like all thymes, will prefer a warm, sunny situation and a well-drained soil, adore inter-planting with some heat-producing pavers in a walkway or such, and appreciate a good mulching of the crowns in winter. There are so many blissful applications for this famously scented herb that I hesitate to offer just one. Rub minced garlic and any of the aforementioned over lamb, pork, or beef roasts, use the garden variety to fragrance a classic tomato sauce, and throw a handful of the lemony sort into an assortment of fresh, steamed, buttered vegetables. Let your imagination guide you to further gastronomic heights.

❦ 73. Wormwood ❦
❦ 74. Southernwood ❦
❦ 75. Mugwort ❦
Artemisia absinthium

Artemisia abrotanum

Artemisia vulgaris

"What saver is better (if physick be true)
For places infected than Wormwood and Rue?
It is a comfort for hart and the braine
And therefore to have it is not in vaine."

—Thomas Tusser, *July's Husbandry*, 1577

The *Artemisia* family, very anciently native to Europe and Asia, is fascinating both herbally and historically—man, it seems, has engaged it an eons-long love-hate relationship, eschewing it for its bitter taste while, at the same moment, swooning over its many "healing" properties. Medicinally, however, this clan has pretty much gone out of favor, so, despite a wealth of fascinating factoids and a bona fide physical comeliness surrounding each of its three main constituents, wormwood (*Artemisia absinthium*), southernwood (*A. abrotanum*), and mugwort (*A. vulgaris*), I have chosen to deal with all of them in this single final chapter. Depending on whom you ask, the family name *Artemisia* derives either from the Greek moon goddess Artemis or from Artemisia, queen of Halicarnassus, who in 353 B.C. built the tomb that would become one of the Seven Wonders of the World for her husband King Mausolous, from which derives the term "mausoleum."

The first historic reference to wormwood (*A. absinthium*) seems to involve the legendary emperor Shen-Nung, father of Chinese agriculture, who reportedly sported the head of a bull on a human form, invented the plow, and, in 2800 B.C., declared that wormwood would cure malaria.

WORMWOOD

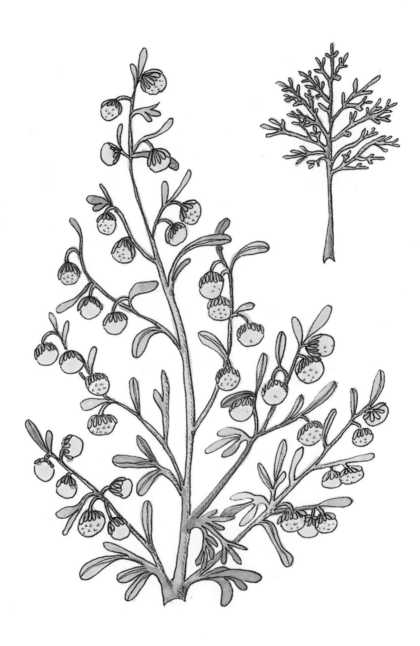

SOUTHERNWOOD

"Wormwood" finds its root in this herb's earliest broad employment as a remedy for intestinal worms, John Gerard noting in his *Herbal* of 1636 that "the plant voideth away worms not only taken inwardly, but applied outwardly," further adding, helpfully, "taken in wine it is good against the biting of the shrew mouse and of the sea dragon." The *absinthium* in wormwood's botanical name comes to us from the Latin *absinthial*, meaning "bitter," which it certainly is, second perhaps only to rue in the nasty-tasting category. Pythagoras claimed wormwood could ease childbirth and Hippocrates recommended it for both menstrual pain and rheumatism, and, for centuries, pungent wormwood was employed as a fumigant and "strewing" herb to banish moths, earning it (and other members of its family) the ancient French appellation *garde-robe* or "clothes-saver." Also famously employed in the manufacture of that near-hallucinatory French experience known as absinthe, wormwood in highly concentrated doses can in fact be poisonous, but in dilutions like teas has proven effective in eliminating worms, increasing stomach acidity, and lowering fevers. However, it is still a rather bitter pill.

Southernwood (*A. abrotanum*) is known by many anciently evocative names, including "Old Man," "Lad's Love," "Our Lord's Wood," and "Maid's Ruin," and, because of its strong camphorlike scent, was also historically employed as both pest deterrent and strewing herb. However, like wormwood, it is seldom used medicinally today except in Germany, generally in a topical poultice for wounds and skin eruptions. Both "Lad's Love" and my favorite antique sobriquet, "Maid's Ruin," are based in three ancient Euro-Mediterranean notions: that southernwood would increase a young man's virility (thus "southern wood"?), was frequently included in the posies young men bestowed upon the maidens they were attempting to seduce, and was also applied lavishly to the cheeks of youths seeking to accelerate manhood by speeding beard growth. John Gerard commented that southernwood "is a gallant Mercurial plant, worthy of more esteem than it has," quoted Dioscorides, who believed, "the seed bruised, heated in warm water, and drank, helps those that are bursten, or troubled with cramps or convulsions of the sinews . . . ," and further added that "the same taken in wine is an antidote, or counter-poison against all deadly poison, and drives away serpents and other venomous creatures . . ." Nicholas Culpeper, while commending it for a panoply of ailments, still returns, however, to that basic herbal hitch: "The whole plant has a nauseous, penetrating, bitter taste."

Mugwort (*A. vulgaris*) has probably grown along the edges of human habitation in Eurasia since we finally sludged out of the muck, its name seeming to come to us from a manhandling of the Old English *moughte* or "moth" into "mug," with the addition of that ancient catch-all for "herbal plant," *wort*, signaling the familiar familial employment as a fragrant insect repellant (interestingly, the Ukrainian word for mugwort is *Chernobyl*). Mugwort was also antiquely known by the charming alias "St. John's Girdle," as St. John the Baptist was said to have worn a girding of mugwort on his journey into the wilderness and, in clear reference to this, John Gerard, quoting Pliny the Elder, reports, "Pliny saith that the traveller or wayfaring man that hath the herbe tied about him feeleth no wearisomnesse at all; and that he who hath it about him can be hurt by no poysonsome medicines, nor by any wilde beast, neither yet by the Sun it selfe . . ." In Pagan ceremony, a modified girdle of mugwort is still worn during the festivities surrounding the summer solstice. At the other end of the herbal-usage spectrum, mugwort has long been a friend to women in terms of childbirth, regulating the menstrual cycle, and easing menopausal symptoms, Culpeper noting, "Mugwort is with good success put among other herbs that are boiled for women to sit over the hot decoction to draw down their courses [and] to help the delivery of their birth . . ." We now know a mild infusion of mugwort can be useful as a digestive stimulant and helpful with mild depression, nervous tension, and anxiety, and, more recently, mugwort and the artemisinin it contains have shown promising antimalarial properties (thank you, Shen-Nung). Still, there's that *bitter* thing . . .

In the end, all three of this chapter's subjects are truly visually appealing shrublike perennials, boasting soft, feathery, sharply fragrant silvery-to-green foliage, small greenish/yellow flowers, and, as you can see, multiple historic herbal applications with a kind of family theme running through them. All are hardy to USDA zone 3 or 4 and are fairly brutally hearty as well, mugwort being so to such an extent that it has naturalized throughout eastern North America and, in North Carolina

MUGWORT

and Virginia, is considered a problematic weed. All are eminently easy to care for when placed in a sunny position, although some, like the beautiful wormwood 'Silver Mound,' will go dormant in the summer heat and then pop right back again when cooler climes return.

A modicum of shapely pruning for all will not go unrewarded: for wormwoods and mugworts, fall is best; for southernwood, snip away in spring or summer. Would I ever ingest any of them? Probably not, but not that I don't believe each could be effective in small doses in the forms of teas and tisanes for their recommended ailments. It really comes down to a taste thing. Therefore, my suggestion is: why not grow some (especially the stunning wormwoods 'Powis Castle' and 'Silver Mound') at the front of your perennial borders for their showstopping silvery presence in the garden as well as that pleasingly camphorlike scent as you brush by?

❦ Bibliography ❦

A Book of Herbs
    Dawn MacLeod
    The Garden Book Club 1968

Aceteria: A Discourse of Sallets (1699)
    John Evelyn
    Brooklyn Botanic Garden 1937

A Garden of Pleasant Flowers (1629)
(Paradisi in Sole Paradisus Terrestris)
    John Parkinson
    Dover Publications 1976

A History of the Vegetable Kingdom
    William Rhind
    Blackie & Son 1865

A Modern Herbal (1931)
    Mrs. M. Grieve
    Dover Publications 1971

An Irish Herbal (1735)
    John K'Eough
    The Aquarian Press 1986

Culpeper's Complete Herbal (1653)
    Nicholas Culpeper
    W. Foulsham & Co., Ltd.

Enquiry Into Plants (third century B.C.)
    Volumes 1 & 2
    Theophrastus
    Harvard University Press 1916

Everyman His Own Gardener
John Abercrombie & Thomas Mawe
Gilbert & Rivington 1834

A Family Herbal
Robert John Thornton
R. & R. Crosby & Co. 1814

Gerard's Herbal (1597)
John Gerard
Spring Books 1927

Herbal Simples
W. T. Fernie
John Wright & Sons 1914

McMahon's American Gardener (1857)
Bernard McMahon
Funk & Wagnalls 1976

Plant Lore, Legends, and Lyrics (1892)
Richard Folkard
Cornell University Library Digital Collections 1992

Sauer's Herbal Cures (1764)
William Woys Weaver
Routledge 2001

Sturtevant's Notes on Edible Plants (1887)
Dr. E. Lewis Sturtevant
(edited by U. P. Hedrick)
New York Agricultural Experiment Station 1919

The American Gardener (1854)
William Cobbett
Kensinger Publishing 2007

The Book of Herbs
    Lady Rosalind Northcote
    John Lane: The Bodley Head 1903

The Complete Book of Herbs
    Leslie Bremness
    Guild Publishing 1990

The English Housewife (1615)
    Gervase Markham
    McGill-Queens University Press 1986

The Folklore of Plants (1889)
    T. F. Thiselton Dyer
    Llanerch 1994

The Illustrated Encyclopedia of Herbs
    Sarah Bunney
    Barnes & Noble 1996

The Meanings of Herbs
    Gretchen Scobel & Ann Field
    Chronicle Books 2001

Thomas Jefferson's Garden Book (1824)
    Thomas Jefferson
    The American Philosophical Society 1944

Wyman's Gardening Encyclopedia
    Donald Wyman
    MacMillan 1971

❧ Resources ❧

5guys.wordpress.com/plant-lore-of-shakespeare
bookofherbs.com
botanical.com
davesgarden.com
gardendigest.com
gardenherbs.org
herbsociety.org
hort.purdue.edu/hort/
hort.oregonstate.edu
magicspells.in.com
quotegarden.com
uchicago.edu
vitaminstuff.com
wikipedia.com